INDIVIDUALISM, COLLECTIVISM, AND POLITICAL POWER

INDIVIDUALISM, COLLECTIVISM, AND POLITICAL POWER

A RELATIONAL ANALYSIS OF IDEOLOGICAL CONFLICT

by

ERVIN LASZLO

THE HAGUE

MARTINUS NIJHOFF

1963

PRINTED IN THE NETHERLANDS

PREFACE

The present study of the interrelation of sociopolitical principles and political power adopts a specific method of construction: it combines philosophical analysis with political facts. The work as a whole belongs neither to the exclusive domain of philosophy, nor to that of political science, but represents a particular combination of some aspects of both fields. It is an attempt to throw some fresh light on the ostensibly irreconcilable ideological East-West conflict by subjecting the characteristic features of basic political thought to a philosophical analysis and then exploring the interpretation of the factual elements of the conflict in terms of its conclusions. Since this project involves the consideration of a highly diversified set of problems, the primary aim was to establish a common frame of reference for the evaluation of the basic elements of the conflict, rather than to treat individual problems in exhaustive detail.

The work is divided into two parts. Part I is devoted first, to the definition of the problem and the designation of the conceptual tools for tackling it, and then, to the systematic, step-by-step construction of a conceptual framework capable of accounting for the conflicting principles of individualism and collectivism by reference to perceptive and cognitive processes, and for the influence of the milieu on the formulation of particular political views and theories. The exploration of the typical structure of historical political theories leads to the consideration of the contemporary forms of Democracy and Communism as coherent resultants of long-term social processes. Part II is consecrated to the analysis of the typical and basic points and process of conflict between individualism and collectivism in their relation to power in contemporary societies.

I wish to express thanks to Prof. J. M. Bochenski for the discussions which helped to crystallize some of the basic ideas of this analysis, to Prof. R. T. De George and to Dr. T. J. Blakeley for reading the manuscript and making valuable suggestions, and to Mr. Peter Beemans for improving the readability of the text. I owe heartfelt gratitude to my wife, who has not only taken over the chores of correcting and typing, but has, with patience and understanding, created an atmosphere conducive to research and creative thought.

Fribourg, Switzerland, June, 1963   E. L.

CONTENTS

PART I

SCHEMATIZATION

INTRODUCTION

(i) *The Problem*

Organized society is built on the assumption that the individual and the collectivity have definite mutual relations, and that most individuals within the social group share a similar conception of this interrelation. It is assumed that every person devotes some thought to his relations to society, or at any rate, that an idea of this relation is implicit in his thinking and behaviour. Contemporary constitutional systems assume further that not only do most individuals within their bounds share a similar conception of their social relations, but that the institutions of state correspond to the view of the majority in this basic respect. Thus, if we define the idea of the relation of the individual to the social collectivity a basic form of political thought, constituted states will be found to *institutionalize* a form or variety of political thinking which, it is assumed, is that of the majority.

The actual correspondence of what we shall term *popular*, and *institutionalized* political thought is, in the last count, the basic factor determining the stability of a state. While government operations and political programmes may diverge from and transcend popular opinion, if salient disagreement obtains on the issue of the individual vs. the collectivity, agreement is impossible on further points. State functions become efficient and effective only when the basic principles they institutionalize are shared (or tolerated, at least) by the representative majority of the people. The likely social processes ensuing when any reformist or revolutionary action programme is introduced may thus be assessed, and the likely development of the forces created by the interaction of institutionalized principles with a living and dynamic social mass become predictable with any amount of certainty, only when the popular political thought typifying the attitude of the greatest masses of the given society is as well known and analysed, as is the idea or theory upon which the programme has been based. In our day, the court of last appeal for every political and social proposition is the political thought of the people. Political power is assured and broken by the coincidence and conflict of the basic premiss of the leadership programme with the premiss of the political thinking of the masses. Totalitarian regimes may remain operative for a time in the face of opposition, but in the long run the reins of power are firmly grasped only by the leader whose political views correspond to, and even anticipate the ideas of the widest population strata.

The contemporary world political scene has become dichotomic, being dominated by two opposing social, economic and political systems. The conflict of Democracy and Communism derives already from a divergent basic premiss concerning the relations of the individual to the collectivity. We maintain that given this divergence all further points conflict, and that the core of the ideological conflict lies therefore in this basic thought. The real, actual scope of the conflict may thus be determined only by studying the penetration of the basic premiss of the institutionalized principles into the social consciousness of the people in the respective blocs.

Such an analysis involves not only thorough sociological and political research, but also a frame of reference common to both of the conflicting parties. The conceptual tools must be developed first: basic political thought must be defined, elaborate social and political schemes must be analysed to a specific variety of this basic premiss, and the mutual influence of institutionalized and popular political thought must be clarified. This is the task set for the first part of this essay.

(ii) The Concepts

The members of primitive tribes, the people of autocratic regimes, totalitarian dictatorships and oligarchies, as well as the citizens of liberal societies imply or express specific opinions as to the nature of their society and tend to advocate particular measures to maintain, reform or radically transform the social order. At first sight the political views of different people in the same societies and of different people in different societies appear to be so diversified as to make a definition applicable to all, a questionable undertaking. When we add to these differences that of time as well, and consider the thought of different people in different historical epochs, then the problem becomes still more complex. Yet if history as a continuous development of generally more cohesive than diversified forces is to make sense, the central dynamism of the process – the political ideas and objectives of different people in all epochs – must be capable of being analysed to common, unifying characteristics and to unchanging components. If we could find the universal human structure of all political thought, we could account for its diversity relationally, and by undertaking a relational analysis, we could see the issues of conflicts and agreements coherently.

The obvious common feature of all political thought is that it deals with society. But society, it may be objected, is a vague concept. Not only do different individuals form divergent ideas of the same society, but society itself is different in different times and places. This contention cannot be countered. As a result the individual's concept of society must be treated as a variable and theoretical concept, and the analysis restricted to a relatively more constant and more immediately knowable element of political thought. Such is the concept of man. Everyone forms an idea of himself and of his fellow beings, as well as of the relations obtaining between them. If human (sense-) experience consists of the perception of objects and their interrelations, experience in the sphere of society may be summarized as the apprehension of individual beings and their social interrelations. The idea of society, notwithstanding its theoretical character, is inferred from the direct experience of the attributes of human beings and of the various types of relations obtaining between them. Thus before we could proceed to a study of the idea of society as it is entertained by different people, we must analyse the possible variants their concepts of man can take. Common to all concepts of man in the context of society are the characteristics of *concreteness* and *relationality*. Man must be considered to be a concrete entity as well as a relational existent, since a conception of society based on either one of these aspects of experience is vacuous: society, pictured as the simultaneous existence of concrete, mutually abstract individual beings is divorced from contemporary social reality, and society as the sum total of existential relations is a purely intellectual, structural concept. The ontological conception of society must include both the concrete subject (individual man as the agent of all social events) and the causal factor of relations (interqualification by virtue of economic, social and cultural relations). Some philosophers find it possible to speak of purely abstract entities, and to posit the unqualified givenness of Being, or else altogether deny the existence of concrete entities and posit merely relations (concrete substance being replaced by nodal points, spatio-temporal events, vacuous actualities, etc.). In social science, however, both a substantial base and a relational structure must be considered. Man cannot be (to use Whitehead's terms) either purely a "subject" or purely a "superject," but must always be both, i.e. a "subject-superject." The ontological concept of man must be based, therefore, on a consideration of the *concrete being* of the individual, as well as on his *relational existence*. The former signifies his individual being, and the latter his relational qualification through social existence.

If society is inferred from the concept of man and the concept of man has these two elemental components, then the idea an individual entertains of society is determined by the combination of the two components in his concept of man. Since individual being and social existence are synthesized in the givenness of each person, they should not be conceived separately, but should be attributed to the very same entity: man. Now there are three combinations of these components possible in an integral, rational and consequent concept of man. (i) Individual being as primary and social existence as secondary, (ii) social existence as primary and individual being as secondary, and (iii) individual being and social existence as qualitatively equal manifestations. If both components are attributed to man, and we hold man to be subject to the laws of causality, some form of causal nexus must obtain between the components. These are as follows: if being is primary and existence secondary, then man's individual being will tend to determine, or at least to mould, the shape of his social existence. Society being the sum total of the social existences of individual beings, it tends to be determined by individuals, in this view. We shall term the idea of society emerging from this concept of man *Individualism*. If social existence is primary and individual being secondary, then the existence of man i.e. his relations to the group, will be determinant of his being. Thus society is seen to mould the individual. This ontological concept of society we shall identify as *Collectivism*.

Should man's individual being and social existence be equal manifestations, then the exigencies of the private being of each man must be held to fully coincide with his socially relevant activities. In order to arrive at this view, we must transcend empirical experience, posit a concept of essence (i.e. individual-social human nature), and deduce from this concept the manifestations of individual being as well as of social existence. While developing a scheme permitting the synthesis of concrete individuality with relational existence appears to be the road to take to the resolution of the conflicts arising from the polar modality of the concept of man, it requires the introduction of further theoretical concepts, and is, for this reason, insufficiently present in the popular notion of society. We shall concentrate here on the idea of society as it is formulated by the great majority of all people, and shall leave the essential argument aside.[1]

As we shall show, the social ontology of every man is disproportionately oriented to the comprehension of being and of existence. Most men tend to regard one or the other component as primal, and hence subordinate the experience of one to the primacy of the other. As a result the representative majority of all people tend either to an individualist or to a collectivist viewpoint. This ontological conception of society is more than an intellectual abstraction – it also enters into the determination of man's actual behaviour in given social situations.

In the last analysis the idea of society is the basis of political action; therein lies the nucleus of political thought and the major cause of the attraction or repulsion of given individuals to specific theories. When the general ontological structure of an institutionalized political theory and the idea of society entertained by the private individual coincide (i.e. when both are based on a concept of man wherein the primacy of the concepts of being and existence is identical), the theory is on the whole – though not necessarily in specific detail – representative of the individual's political thinking and may be accepted by him without raising *major* objections. When such a coincidence is not given, the theory appears unacceptable, although its acceptance remains pending upon the shift of emphasis in the individual's mind concerning the primacy of the ontological concepts of individual being and social existence. (It is one of the aims of this work to inquire into the possibilities of producing such a shift by means of a totalitarian ideological campaign.)

We shall use the term "political thought" to denote the conceptual foundation of rational policies and schemes involving several individuals in an organized collectivity. We shall make use of the controversial term "ideology" as well, understanding thereunder political

---

[1] For an essential interpretation of man, cf. this author's *Essential Society*, The Hague, 1963.

thought which is (a) *systematic* – using its basic ontological structure to substantiate all its premisses, (b) *holistic* – using this structure to interpret not only man and society, but general reality as well, (c) *propagated* – being adopted by an organ of political power to infuse its idea of society among wide layers of the population, (d) *institutionalized* – being used as blueprint for the building or rebuilding of society concordantly with its ontological premiss. Inasmuch as not only ideologies, but also liberal political schemes are based on a specific conception of man, a general interaction obtains between the political thought of every society's representative majority and its insti-tutionalized political principle. Each individual political scheme derives from the thinker's actual experience, and is therefore the product of its times, while all political thought is influenced by the institutionalized application of a rationalized scheme. Hence the political thought obtaining in society is always the product of histori-cal-social conditions, plus the effect of the political principle of the government. This principle itself may be the product of local historical-social conditions, but is not necessarily that – political principles can be imported as well as exported. The resultant of ideological power-politics may the transformation of a people's ontological concept of society, notwithstanding eventual disparities between the particular theory and the history of political thought in that nation. There is a two-fold interaction shaping the evolution of contemporary political thought: on the one hand there is the interaction of local sociological conditions and the people's idea of society, and on the other the inter-action between an institutionalized *a priori* ideology and the existent political thought of the population. In the free world only the first kind of interaction obtains – this is one, and perhaps the major justi-fication of the predicate "freε" with respect to liberal societies. Where-ever Soviet power penetrates, however, the second form of interaction is superimposed on the first: the Communist ideology's ontological structure comes to act on the political thought of the people, and, together with the full-scale reconstruction of the social order, helps to emphasize the primacy of social existence over individual being concurrently with the collectivist structure of the ideology.

While we uphold the idea that every body of political thought is valid only in the particular historical context which has given rise to it, we do not deny the possibility of a historically-socially foreign theory flourishing for a time by virtue of being applied and propagated by totalitarian methods. The interaction of preconceived schemes and living political thought is essentially dynamic: the scheme can change actual conditions, although it is not immune from the influences of changing conditions itself. The dynamic interplay of institutionalized and popular political thought forms a continuous dialogue which becomes meaningful only if both poles are considered. Political thought, even in the highly explicated and systematized form of social and political philosophy, differs from other bodies of thought precisely in that political thought derives from actual conditions, acts on actual conditions, and is in turn influenced by the dynamics of changing conditions, while systems of thought which deal with less pliant topics, or with universal and ideal objects and relations, are proportionately less exposed to the influence of the milieu of the thinker.

Notwithstanding the close involvement of political thought with the observation and categorization of partially unverifiable elements (the eternal "ghost in the machine" of man and society), all varieties of political thought can be analysed to common components. These are the components of the empirical concept of man: *individual being,* as "subject" and *social existence,* as "superject".[1]

---

[1] Whitehead defines "subject" as "a moment of the genesis of self-enjoyment. It consists of a purposed self-creation out of materials which are at hand in virtue of their publicity". A "superject" on the other hand "arises from the publicity which it finds, and it adds itself to the publicity which it transmits. It is a moment of passage from decided public facts to a novel public fact". A. N. Whitehead, *Process and Reality,* Part IV, Chapter I, Section V.

THE EPISTEMOLOGICAL BASES OF THE
CONCEPT OF MAN

(i) *The Premisses*

In this chapter we submit to analysis the subject-object relations leading to the formulation of the concept of man. The definition of this concept – which we hold to be the nucleus of political thought – follows through basic modes of perceiving, apprehending and comprehending external reality. We shall attempt to trace differences obtaining in concepts of man formulated by different individuals to the knowing process itself, or more precisely, to the intellectual approach of the knowing mind to the known object. An ontological analysis of political thought presupposes as a consequence an epistemological argument (or at least the clarification of the epistemological premisses) no less than any other thesis dealing with the analysis or evaluation of any aspect of reality.

The epistemological problem has proved to be insurmountable since the Cartesian formulation of the ego-centric predicament. Every attempt to transcend the vicious circle of the knowing mind and its apperceptive states demands the inclusion of some contingent elements into the argument. The certainty of knowing the world as given and as it might be known by an uncorporeal omnipresent Being has vanished, and given place to admittedly speculative inferences about the most likely nature of reality. The prime source of contention is the suitability of methods and approaches for the acquisition of knowledge of optimal (but not absolute) truth-value. The discoveries and theorems of modern science have further removed any doubt that may have existed as to the absolute reliability of sense-data: sense-data taken on face value, may evidently be fallible.

Notwithstanding the increasing epistemological barrier between absolute knowledge and objective reality, man's thirst for knowledge has not abated but has, on the contrary, intensified in the past centuries. The presence of the epistemological problem has merely led to the adoption of nominalism in the investigations of the natural sciences. Objective being became a speculative concept, left out of consideration wherever possible. It *is* possible to pursue research in the natural sciences nominalistically, without making statements about the objective "being" of the subject matter. Such methods are not possible, however, in the immediate sphere of experience. Everyday experience cannot be nominalistically restricted, since common sense normally (and for ordinary existence, necessarily) assumes that familiar objects are independently existent in the form in which they are apprehended. The objective, real being of man is implicit in the idea of society as popularly formulated, in some form or another. The attributes of the objective reality of man may be defined on the basis of a study of his general anthropological and particular psychological characteristics, as well as through the study of his relations to other men and his activity and behaviour in a social context. The definition of man's objective givenness can be approached from two viewpoints, but both approaches result in a concept which is not nominalistic but essential. Since this concept, purporting to be an objective definition of man's reality, is based on the interpretation of empirical sense-data, and sense-data are considered fallible, the concept of man is in fact a nominal concept functioning as an essential one in the context of political thought. There are no means of verifying the one-to-one correspondence of the concept of man to objective reality, yet this concept is operative as the centre of consistent social behaviour and political action. However, in the final analysis absolute verification is impossible not only with respect to the concept of man, but with respect to *all* concepts, regardless whether they function as nominal descriptions or as essential definitions. In our view concepts are contingent and speculative means of breaking away from the ego-centric predicament – nevertheless, they prove to be an effective and operative means. Rejecting this epistemological standpoint of conceptual nominalism necessarily leads to dogmatic realism or to agnostic scepticism. We find dogmatism in political thought in the form of an assertion of unconditional validity for a specific concept of man, while agnosticism is excluded from the realm of actual politics, since some knowledge of man and society (functioning as a set of essential concepts) must be at hand to provide the ground for any kind of political attitude – notwithstanding the refusal of antievaluationists to admit an essentialistic interpretation of social processes.

We shall treat the essential concept of man as nominal rather than real in this argument, and examine the various characteristics attributed by different concepts to man, without positing the unconditional and absolute truth-value of either. Regardless, however, whether the particular features of our epistemological theorem are accepted or not (for several theories of knowledge may arrive at the fundamentally same ontological conclusion), its postulate remains uneffected: that the concept of man may be formulated on the basis of objective as well as subjective comprehensional processes, and that in popular political thought either an objective or a subjective process predominates at the expense of the other.

(ii) The Knowledge of Individual Being and Social Existence

Increasing evidence for the common origin of all entities and their temporal-spatial rather than qualitative subsequent differentiation makes a transcendental standpoint in epistemology superfluous: the knowing subject and the known object may be held to exist on the same four-dimensional plane. Consequently we shall adopt here an immanent viewpoint, but will restrict the analysis to the consideration of particular objects, excluding universals from the discussion. The ideal entities of logic and mathematics will be outside the scope of our inquiry; we are dealing with ontologically existent, real and contingent objects only. Similarly excluded from the discussion will be all psychological factors deriving from a consideration of apperceptive processes. The relations that we wish to examine are those between the subject (considered as a psycho-physical, organic totality) and the object (any existent entity, animate or inanimate, capable of affording sense-data).

We shall distinguish three functional processes as the basis of ontological concepts. The first of these is *perception*.

By perception we mean purely sensory perception, a process whereby sense-data reach a sense-organ and are registered by it, i.e. produce a neuro-physical chain process leading the corresponding sensation from the sense-organ to the brain. For example, a red dot is presented to the subject, that is, the sense-data which produce the sensation of redness and roundness of a particular size, reach the subject's eye. In ordinary conditions of perception this red dot is not the only percept within a person's visual range, and the eye is not the only organ transmitting sensations. By the mere sense-perception of the red dot we mean simply the fact that the sense-data of redness and roundness are presented to the eye, and are registered by it. They do not reach consciousness as the idea of a red dot, however, unless they are not only perceived, but also apprehended.

Apprehension is the second stage in the relation of objects to consciousness. Apprehension in our use will signify an act of consciousness on the part of the subject, an act whereby the object enters the range of the conscious mind. The act involves the awareness of the presence of the object, but this awareness is as yet bare, it is exclusive of any judgment. An apprehended object may, on the other hand, be remembered and associated with other apprehensions. It is not evaluated either in its actually perceived, or in its remembered form. To return to our example: the percept registered as a red dot reaches consciousness as a specific form and colour among the several shapes, sizes, colours, sounds, tastes, etc. which the senses perceive and transmit to the brain. The person is aware of a red dot but does not know what it is (the effort to find our more about it is not to be included under the act of apprehension). Apprehension signifies merely the conscious awareness of a particular conformation of percepts among the manifold signals received through the senses.

Comprehension is the third and highest stage in this subject-object relation. When data are apprehended, i.e. when perceived data reach consciousness, their comprehension may take place. A given portion of apprehended data must be comprehended in order to insure the subsistence of the organism. Above and beyond this, comprehension serves the satisfaction of the intellect. It is a reasonable proposition that while most animals attain some form of comprehension of environmental objects, man alone comprehends a sphere of reality extending considerably beyond the realm of objects necessary for his subsistence. We shall examine here the problem of how objects (meaning always real, particular existents) are comprehended.

Objects of a *vital* significance (those that permit the subsistence of the individual) are in a direct, pragmatic contact with the individual some time during his existence. Such contact is in most cases periodic. Hence when a vital object (such as food) is not in an actual contact with the subject (i.e. when it is not actually eaten) it must nevertheless be recognized (as an eatable object). This much, we may assume, is also the case with animals. The process, in our view, is primarily conceptual: pragmatic experience affords certain sensations, and the object becomes associated with these sensations even when the sensations are not present (i.e. when the food is not actually eaten). A concept is assigned thereby to the object which incorporates the sensations; in other words the concept infuses the meaning of the sensations into the apprehension of the object's sense-data. Since vital sensations are meaningful, *comprehensible* to the subject, the conception of an object as capable of yielding such sensations, makes its data comprehensible. Hence when an object is presented, which memory associates with vital sensations, the object appears to be potentially (even if not actually) productive of these sensations. The object is seen as an entity that produces these particular sensations: the object is denoted by a corresponding predicate signifying the potency of the object to produce such sensations. The predicate affords the comprehension of the object and this predicate is the object's *concept*.

Such "vital" concepts apply to all objects capable of producing correspondingly vital sensations; to all objects that is, which contribute in some way to the subsistence and well-being of the subject. However, the sphere of such objects may be extended almost *ad infinitum* in the case of civilized man. Objects which do not actually contribute to his basic, animal subsistence can be seen as contributing to his civilized existence, by satisfying if not a physical, then an intellectual requirement. Hence, an object which in no way contributes to the subject's subsistence, (such as a painting for example) can be seen as contributing instead to his intellectual requirement. Certain objects can be better or more readily comprehended in the context of existential relevance than others. A starry sky may be poetically comprehended as an object of beauty (thus giving intellectual satisfaction and becoming relevant to the subject's existence), it may also be comprehended as a source of light on an unlit path (being relevant to the subject's physical requirements), nevertheless civilized men comprehend stars most often as distant stellar bodies. With that we come upon an entirely different mode of comprehension.

Comprehending a twinkling light on the night sky as a distant stellar body of unimaginably large dimensions is also to conceptualize it. Yet the concept has, in this case, been derived from measurements of the given sense-data and from subsequent mathematical calculations. These were communicated as true, permitting now the comprehension of star light as a stellar unit, by all "knowing" people. Aside from the inferentiality of such comprehensions (which is typical of all comprehensions of the mode we are now discussing) a basic difference between comprehension of the star as an object of beauty or source of light on the way, and as a stellar body, is that in the two former events sense-data are comprehended as belonging to an object relevant to the subject's existence (understanding under the term existence also subsistence, i.e. both physical and intellectual satisfactions) while in the latter event the sense-data are comprehended without bringing the object into a pragmatic relational contact with the subject: the star as a stellar body is understood in its own right, as an independently existent object.

Let us see how such a comprehension is possible. A star (or any other object) may be comprehended as an independent object if we understand the properties which the object possesses. A star understood as a mass of rocks is comprehended by its solidity: a pragmatic property. The star comprehended as a ball of fire is again understood by virtue of a pragmatic property (heat). When a physicist comprehends a star he does so by deducing from its pragmatic properties certain processes not available to the senses in themselves (such as the proton-proton cycle, for example). Nevertheless the comprehension has followed a deduction from empirical properties, capable of being pragmatically experienced. Consequently, the star as a stellar body is comprehended as the sum total of in themselves pragmatic qualities. These qualities are abstracted then from the context of actual experience and attributed to the object. There is a process of abstraction present here which is missing in the formerly discussed mode of comprehension. There, the object was comprehended as actually relevant to the subject. Here, on the other hand, the object is understood to exist in its own right, its relevance to the subject is not considered (or if it is, it does not determine or change the process of its comprehension); the object is seen as an independent entity incorporating in its being a bundle of pragmatic properties.

There are, in this mode of comprehension as well, various grades of ease obtaining in comprehending objects of the immediate environment and objects of a wider sphere of reality. Here the grading is inverted, however: the more removed an object is, the easier it is to abstract it from the vital sphere of the subject's existence, and the more readily it is comprehended as an independent and real object. The closer the object is to the vital sphere of the subject's existence, the more difficult this abstraction becomes. It is nevertheless possible to abstract a vital object in frequent pragmatic relation with the subject from the context of the subject's existence, and to comprehend it as independently real: an apple, for example, may be seen as the product of a species of trees, growing under given conditions and at certain times, while by deduction the apple may even be considered as a molecular compound, or as an atomic complex. The most frequent concept of the apple (the concept to which the word refers in its everyday use) is *food*, however, a vital concept, relevant to the subject's existence.

In carrying the above argument further, it becomes evident that almost every complex of sense-data may be comprehended by two basic modes of comprehension: (a) as the sum total of properties representing a specific degree of relevance for the subject's existence, and (b) as the sum total of properties given in themselves. Now these two modes of comprehension are marked by definite distinguishing characteristics. Objects comprehended as the sum total of relevant properties signify a *subjective* mode of comprehension: the object is evaluated in the context of the subject's relations to his environment. The object is denoted by the subject as the opposite pole of the subject-object relation. Its individual, independent characteristics are ignored, or else play a secondary role, for the object is seen as the sum total of actual or potential sensations. Consequently not the object's but the *subject's* properties have been instrumental in assigning the concept through which comprehension takes place. The comprehension results from the cognition of the relation of the object to the subject, and is evaluated correspondingly to the subject's existential needs and requirements. In this event the object is understood as being *relationally real*.

Now objects comprehended as *independently real* signify an *abstraction* of their inferred properties from the subject's sphere of existence. The object is understood as the sum total of relevant properties, grouped in a complex which itself exists, regardless of its relevance. The properties are abstracted from the context of the subject's existence, and are attributed exclusively to the object. In this mode of comprehension the properties of the *object* have been instrumental for assigning a concept to the object, permitting thereby its comprehension. Consequently this mode of comprehension can be termed *objective*.

Thus we have two basic modes of comprehension: the subjective and the objective. The subjective mode of comprehension emphasizes the relational properties of phenomena; the objective mode accentuates their concrete givenness. Environmental objects are more readily comprehended as relationally real, while objects that are more removed from man's daily existence are usually comprehended as independently real. The subjective mode of comprehension is characterized by a greater measure of concentration on the immediate means and ends of subsistence, and the objective mode signifies greater intellectual powers.

How these modes of comprehension result in a knowledge of "being" and "existence" in the sense in which these terms are defined here, may be clarified as follows: The subjective mode of comprehension treats objects as relationally real, as relevant to the subject's existence. Now existence signifies in our usage that mode of man's givenness which consists of interaction with environmental entities. The actual range, as well as the selection of entities for environmental interaction is largely determined by the type of entities and the pattern of inter-relations characterizing a given position in the social order. Most man have those objects and those persons for interactive partners which their social position designates, and makes available for them. Thus "existence" for man is intimately bound up with social position – existence is ultimately, *social* existence. Thus when environmental reality is comprehended in terms of interrelations, society, and perhaps nature also, is evaluated in the context of social existence: sub-jective comprehension means comprehension from a given social standpoint.

In contrast to this, the objective mode of comprehension abstracts cognized objects from the sphere of the subject's existence, and understands them as independently real. Hence when we exclude consideration of an object's external coordinations, and treat it as a concrete entity existent in itself, we typify the resultant concepts of objective comprehensional processes by the term "individual being." When we comprehend a person objectively, we attempt to understand him as he is in himself, through taking account of his various proper-ties, physical, intellectual, and psychological qualities. We exclude from the process of comprehension all consideration of relational coordinations between subject and object. The briefest resumé of the argument would state that objective comprehension is the evaluation of the social environment as a realm of individual beings.

Yet the concept of man can neither be *purely* relational nor *purely* concrete, but must be both. We cannot consider man in an exclusively functional context, i.e. as corresponding to our needs of existence and nothing more: each man evidently has an individual being as well, which is abstract from (though perhaps not irrelevant to) our own existence. Conversely we cannot see other men in our environment as individuals who are entirely irrelevant to our existence, for we relate to them, gain the means of livelihood through them, and obtain most of the necessities of life through their labour. Hence a (social) *existence* as well as an (individual) *being* must be posited for each person, notwithstanding that the concepts of being and existence derive from dissimilar modes of comprehension.

It should be evident from the above discussion that persons who are unable to abstract their thoughts from the context of their own needs and desires tend to consider man as a primarily relational entity – a social existent – for it is through the various relations obtaining between the subject and other members of his community that such needs are fulfilled. On the other hand persons with a profound disregard for their own socially obtainable satisfactions would tend to view men as abstract entities – individual beings – attributing all experienced qualities of individuals to their own being, without permitting the subject-object relation to influence their definition of the concept. Although such an assumption has a broad general validity, the definition of the concept of man is subject to particular historical, social and political influences which must be studied before conclusions as to the person's idea of society can be reached.

There is a double sequence of comprehensional processes conditioning the definition of every concept: the temporal sequence of *successive* comprehensions attained by the individual; and the spatial sequence of *simultaneous* comprehensions obtaining in a collectivity. The former results in the individual's general conceptual view of reality, both in the sphere of society and in that of nature, while the latter signifies the conditioning effect of the dominant species of viewpoints in a collectivity upon the individual's ideas of societal and general reality.

It is interesting to note in this context that, if we assume that individuals employ a typically relational mode of comprehension we will arrive at the conclusion that the content of consciousness is essentially *social* (since whatever is comprehended is always evaluated in the framework of its application to a personal requirement, and such requirements vary with the social position of the individual); while proceeding on the basis of the assumption that individuals make use of typically abstract, objective comprehensional processes the argument will take us to the proposition that the individual's personal standpoint in society has little effect upon his acquisition of knowledge, hence we will conclude that the content of consciousness is primarily personal, and social only insofar as "personal" signifies also "generally human" and is thus applicable in essence to the collectivity as well. According to our thesis, however, consciousness must be regarded as having both a social and a personal content, the proportion of the elements being determined by whether relational, or abstract modes of comprehension dominate the conceptual apparatus of the individual.

THE CONCEPTUAL CONTENT OF THE
IDEA OF REALITY

The premiss adopted in this epistemological argument is that the bases of comprehension are the particular subject-object relations, established through the sensory perception, conscious apprehension and conceptual comprehension of the sense-data attributed to the object. This strictly empirical base is further qualified by a series of influences external to the given subject-object relation. Each particular subject-object relation and each particular concept derived from the cognitive processes based on that relation, forms one part of the general outlook on reality of the individual (his *Weltanschauung* in an ontological sense), and is seen in the light of the individual's over-all approach to his experience of reality, being treated by his already developed conceptual apparatus, while at the same time further developing it. This basic thesis would no doubt be sufficient to evolve a general epistemological theory, capable of shedding light on the problems that occupied the minds of most philosophers since the time of Descartes, Leibnitz, Locke, Hume, and Kant. The purpose of the present work is a much more modest one, however. Our intention is to deal merely with the cognitive processes which play a predominant role in the ontological evaluation of societal (and by implication, of general) reality, and which may thus be shown to have influenced the political thought of our contemporaries. We shall restrict the scope of the argument to dealing with the typical features of a kind of thinking which is essentially action-bound. Having outlined the perceptive processes at its base, our next task is to examine its content, by determining the ontological status of the resulting concepts. The concept is the *content* of the comprehension, for it is the sum total of properties attributed to the object. Although the concept may be derived from seeing the object as a relationally as well as an independently real entity, the object is always seen as one part or aspect of a category of

things external to the subject. The concept is the means of comprehending this part or aspect of external things, and thus the concept
carries the weight of the assumption of correspondence to reality: the
concept has an ontological truth-value. Having assumed the sceptical
epistemological position of conceptual nominalism we do not inquire
into the validity of the concept's truth-value, nor does this validity
interest our argument. Our thesis is that there are two types of concepts
ascribable to every apprehended object, resulting from two different
modes of comprehending it. Forcing the issue on a conceptually
realistic premiss we would be obliged to consider one of these true and
the other false. However, (aside from the fact that such a clear-cut
distinction signifies dogmatism in ontological arguments) our purpose
is not to reach absolutes, but to investigate the genesis and qualification of the patterns of ontological concepts. Thus we shall take the
truth-value of a concept as relative to the mode of comprehension
from which it results, and disregard whether or not it corresponds
one-to-one to "absolute reality".

Concepts derive from the relation of subject to object. The relation
may be conceptualized subjectively or objectively, depending on
whether a property of the subject or of the object has been instrumental
in the comprehension.

If we increase the scope of our analysis and include into our thesis
the *sequence* of comprehensions performed by one subject, the per-
sistent unity of one pole – that of the subject – introduces a source
of influence acting upon each single act of comprehension and deriving
from previous acts; the individual's comprehension of particular
sense-data is conditioned by the sum total of his past comprehensions.
The continuous comprehensional activity of the individual, prompted
by the concrete needs of physical subsistence and by intellectual
endeavours, develops a conceptual apparatus of the mind, which is
engaged every time an object is comprehended. The general orientation
of the apparatus determines whether a majority of objective comprehensions takes place, or whether subjective ones predominate. (The
apparatus itself is subject to the conditioning effect of diverse factors,
with which we shall deal subsequently.) The structure of the apparatus
is such that it makes use of objective and subjective comprehensional
processes. This becomes evident if we consider that in order to obtain
a purely subjective structure we would have to infer all objects from
our own existence, while to have an objective comprehension-mass we
could not do otherwise but deduce concepts from the pure givenness

of objects. We cannot engage in purely subjective comprehensions any more than we can make exclusive use of objective ones. When we speak of orientation, therefore, we assume that one or the other mode of comprehension sufficiently predominates in the conceptual apparatus of the individual to produce an idea of general reality, which tends to attain comprehensions of the objects of empirical experience either through the existence of the subject, or through the being of objects. In practice this is evidently the case.

The point we wish to emphasize here, is that the general content of the idea of reality oriented toward the subjective mode of comprehension yields an ontological conception of the world as relevant to the subject's existence – every act of comprehension performed on that principle helps further to illuminate the nature and properties of the subject, and by inference, of man in general. The resultant of such an orientation is a general *ontology of existence*, more or less complete, according to the intellectual capacities of the subject. The predominant content of an objectively oriented idea of reality will be an *ontology of being*, on the other hand. There every act of comprehension serves to add a further concept to the general conception of objective reality, and further to clarify thereby the ontology of the world of perceived and apprehended sense-data. The two ontologies differ not only in content, but also in susceptibility to human conditioning factors. This latter difference derives from the fact that objective comprehensions may involve all concrete properties of the object, but only the conceptual apparatus (and not the concrete factors of existence) of the subject, while subjective comprehensions may involve any of the concrete existential factors of the subject, and only relevant the sense-data of the object.

Comprehension involves the subject-object relation in both subjective and objective processes. In an objective process comprehension follows through finding a correspondence between the being of the subject (i.e. those of his properties which make up his independent reality) and the manifest properties of the object: once discovered, these properties are attributed to the independent reality, i.e. the *being*, of the object. A property of the object, then, which is common to both the object and subject regardless of the relationship obtaining between them, is instrumental to attaining comprehension. In a subjective comprehensional process, however, the object is understood in the context of the sensations it produces upon the subject when a pragmatic relation occurs. The independent reality of the object is not analysed; the object is evaluated as a functor of the subject's external coordinations. Hence the decisive factor in objective comprehensions is the sense-data of the object, while in subjective comprehensions that factor is the existential requirements of the subject (and of man in general). This distinction assumes primary importance when we consider the influences acting upon each individual and conditioning the conceptual content of his idea of reality. The component of that idea which we have termed an "ontology of being" appears thus to be directly determined by the apprehension of sense-data. Insofar as these data may be verified by the introduction of units of measurement, and by the comparison of the observations of different individuals, the property of objects through which objective comprehensions are effected can be checked, and *individual* bias, at any rate, can be cancelled out.

In subjective processes, however, the desicive factor of comprehension is an existential requirement of the subject.

Existential requirements are not constant as sense-data are, nor can they be checked by any unit of measurement. Such requirements are products of changing conditions, and can make the comprehension of the same object yield different concepts at different times and places, since conditions (and hence requirements) change from time to time and from place to place. Inasmuch as the object is evaluated in the context of the subject's existence the concept assigned to the object will correspond to the subject's requirements (and be variable, therefore) and not to its being (which affords constant sense-data). Let us illustrate this with an example. A house comprehended by virtue of one of its own properties yields the same concept as long as its sense-data are constant. Understood as a structure of stone and brick, or as a molecular or atomic complex, the house is a verifiable "fact"; differences of perception arising from the position, or mental and physical conditions of the subject can be subjected to measurements, notes compared and individual bias cancelled out. The property of the house (let us say the solidity of the brick of which it is constructed) has been the decisive factor of the comprehension; this is a property of the house's independent reality – its "being" – comprehended through common elements with the independent reality of the subject – the subject's being. We then consider the eventuality that the house is comprehended subjectively. In that case the house is comprehended by virtue of its relevance to a requirement of the subject, i.e. to his requirement of being sheltered, having a home, etc.

Although every man requires home and shelter, different men have different preconceptions of what a home and shelter *is*. When a man apprehends a house, his comprehension of the house *qua* home is influenced by his existential conditions: e.g. whether he (or the subject whom he has in mind, be it an individual or merely the idea of man in general) finds the house desirable. The requirement by which the house is comprehended may also be *negative*, in the event, for example, that the house is a prison. The house would still be comprehended by virtue of a requirement, but by a negative one in that case: the prison is to be avoided or escaped from. In a subjective comprehension the object is always comprehended correspondingly to the subject's existential requirement, as good or as bad, beautiful or ugly, a castle or a prison. The predication, as the designation, is determined by the relevance of the object to a specific requirement of the subject. Hence we can advance the proposition that an objective comprehension is not necessarily subject to determination by the observer's existential conditions (if it is influenced by these, the bias may be cancelled out again), while a subjective comprehension is made possible by generic existential requirements and the resulting concept is determined by the particular features of the subject's specific conditions.

When we take the sequence of comprehensions of an individual and consider the influence of each comprehension on all successive ones, we find that an individual acquires an idea of reality oriented toward (but not exclusively composed of) either a subjective or an objective mode of comprehension. In each case he develops an ontology which reflects the modes of comprehension he has used. A subjectively oriented individual's idea of reality is dominated by his ontology of existence, an existence which is variously affected by different external relations functioning as factors of the determination of his particular state. In an objectively oriented person's idea of reality the world of objective entities is predominant, and he interprets his own being in the context of the common factors underlying being in general. While one or the other component predominates, the integral ontology of every man is an intermixture of the two: some aspects of reality are comprehended in the context of human existence, while some others through the sense-data's objective givenness.

The characteristic of the objective portion of the individual's general ontology is that it is relatively (and in potential absolutely) free of individual bias, while the subjective section is inextricably bound up with the specific existential factors of the person. We do not propose value-judgments here, however. "Objective" and "subjective" are used as terms designating a specific process of comprehension, and not as implying the desirability or superiority of one over the other. While an existential ontology may be as valid as an objective one, on the basis of the above argument the proposition can nevertheless be advanced that the former is subject to the conditioning influence of factors which arise from individual situations, while the latter is only subject to the general limitations of the human condition.

THE STRUCTURE OF POLITICAL THEORIES

Political thought, the topic of our essay, can now be reintroduced through a discussion of its components. Political thought deals with the sphere of human society, hence it must be based on some kind of *knowledge* of society. Now society can be conceived from either one of two points of views: from that of the individual, or from that of the collectivity. None of the two poles can be taken independently of the other, for neither is society merely the contemporaneous existence of independent individuals, nor is it merely the existence of a collective social body. The aspect of the individual, as that of the group must be taken into account. The importance a person attaches to the individual and to the collective factor determines his political standpoint within the two extremes of this necessary polarity. While it may also be held that the maximum well-being of the individual and the group coincide, the political means of attaining this utopian society follow either by adjusting the existence of the individual to fit the group (the socialist idea) or adjusting the existence of the group to fit the being of the individual (the liberal idea). Political thought concerns society, hence it deals with individual being *and* with social existence. Since political thinking presupposes a knowledge of both aspects of man's givenness, sufficient ontological concepts must be developed to permit the study of man as an individual and as a socially existent entity.

On the basis of direct sense-experience the external world may be understood either as a world of objective being or as the relevant sphere of human (essentially social) existence. Contemporary man employs both modes in his life, and as a result he develops a general ontology having two different types of concepts as content: concepts of being, through which he regards objects as well as himself as individual beings of given characteristics, keeping individual identities separate even in interrelational processes; and concepts of existence, through which the extraneous world appears as a source of various levels and forms of satisfaction for intrinsic human requirements. These two ontologies involve the person's environment, hence many objects are bound to be common to both.

Since some objects are comprehended and perhaps even predicated objectively as well as subjectively, an inherent schism would develop in the person's idea of reality, unless one faction comes to dominate the other sufficiently to resolve the conflict of divergent concepts, resulting from different modes of comprehension. In fact, one or another ontology predominates in every person's general ontology to the point where the contrary elements disappear as disturbing factors from conscious thought. We can speak of a general orientation of the person either toward subjective comprehensions and the world of existence, or toward objective comprehensions and the world of being.

The idea of society manifests this modal polarity. Political thought, if it is content with a few general observations and uncoordinated judgments of different aspects of the social scene, may be derived directly from the ontology of the person, attained purely by empirical means, through experience. But if political thought attempts to be systematic, and coordinates its judgments into a unilateral framework serving as criterion, then the two types of ontological concepts of all empirical *Weltanschauungs* have to be tuned to a common principle. Being and existence can be brought into a common formula by interpretations, i.e. by adding theoretical concepts to permit an integral heuristic analysis of the concepts of being and the concepts of existence.

Now these heuristically functioning theoretical concepts must also derive from some aspect of empirical experience. The heuristic concept can be a purely relational formula only if the natural orientation of the person's idea of reality is transcended, and he acknowledges the identity of being and existence.[1] We advance the proposition that the heuristic concepts of contemporary political theories are derived either from an ontology of being, or from one of existence, and subordinate one set of concepts to the other correspondingly. In the last analysis contemporary political theories represent the systematization

---

[1] A heuristic concept relating equally to both ontologies may be developed if each person is taken simultaneously as socially existent and individually being. This is possible if we evolve an organic ontology wherein each being is the sum total of socially existing components. Man is then viewed as a being arising through the social existence (organic interfunctioning) of his elements (organs, cells, molecules, atoms) and society is conceived of as a being constituted by the social interrelations (in the sense of organic interfunctioning) of individual being-existences, i.e. persons. cf. *Essential Society op. cit.*

of some already existent ideas of social and general reality. They hypostatize the thinker's predominant mode of thinking, by resolving all conflicts between empirical evidence and preconceived intellectual ideas through the use of concepts by means of which actual experience can be evaluated in the light of his general approach to reality.

Political theories (as the systematically integrated form of the polar ideas of society) take position with respect to the modal polarity of ontological knowledge, and may be criticised as giving priority either to concepts of social existence or to those of individual being. Theories built upon an ontology of being consider each object in terms of its own properties rather than in terms of interrelations. Political theories of this kind emphasize the individual being of man, and envisage a society built upon the rights and freedom of the individual. The position of the person in the social order is seen to correspond to his being rather than to his existence. If the conception of being distinguishes different grades, so it will envisage a hierarchy of rights and degrees of freedom as well. If the quality of being is held to be equal for all men, the rights and freedom of all will be equal also. Theories of this kind systematize the *individualist* idea of society.

Theories based on an ontology of existence, on the other hand, take men in the context of social relevance and consider their existential relations to be those of essentially social entities. These theories develop a concept of man wherein he appears as the sum total of his existential relations, a sum which corresponds, and is determined by, the totality of relations in his collective group.[1] Hence in the existential context men are seen as parts or members of an economic and cultural collectivity, and their personalities identified with the standpoint they occupy in it. Theories built on the ontology of existence represent the systematization of the *collectivist* idea of society.

It should be noted here that, since the existential ontology is liable to determination by the social milieu of the subject, while whatever influences act on an ontology of being may be (potentially at least) eliminated, and reduced to the level of the generic subjectivity of the human condition, political theories based upon existential concepts (collectivist theses) are exposed to the influence of the milieu of the thinker directly, with no possibility of eliminating this influence through

---

[1] Not only relations between men, but also the relations of men to other objects are subsumed here; the social relations of civilization as well as the material relations of subsistence are to be understood under the term "existential relations."

comparative verification; while theories based upon concepts of being (individualist theses) are not necessarily influenced by the conditions of the thinker, at least insofar as their concepts of being are concerned. When we consider that for a full understanding of man both his being and his existence must be comprehended, and that contemporary theories subordinate one to the other, we shall come to the conclusion that collectivist theories derive from a comprehension of existence, and thus may be able to deal with its problems in the immediate sphere of the thinker's experience (but not necessarily elsewhere), and individualist theories may have universal validity, but are likely to fail to provide for a full grasp of the pattern of existence in specific societal situations, since they tend to subordinate actual existential experience to a general conception of man's being.

HISTORICAL-SOCIAL INFLUENCES IN THE STRUCTURE OF POLITICAL THEORIES

Political and social theories differ from popular political thought only in that they are systematic, i.e. they represent an idea of society which is, if not actually deduced from an integral idea of reality, at least not overtly contradicting it. An individual may think of society subjectively and of general reality objectively, or *vice versa;* but political theories are obliged to harmonize their idea of society with their conception of reality in general. Such an integral systematization is not always explicitly undertaken, although an understanding of society is implicit in every political theory, and such understanding implies a comprehension of general reality as the setting for social events. Marx and Engels, for example, formed an idea of society and realized the need to bring it in harmony with general reality. Consequently Engels applied the principle categories of Marx's social thesis to the interpretation of nature. Most other political theories are content with tacit implications which are nevertheless capable of being explicated *post factum*, by deduction, once the theory is presented.

Political theories represent the systematic elaboration of the thinker's idea of society. Since this idea includes a comprehension of individual being and of social existence, political theories are exposed to the influence of the milieu: concepts of being may be immune from the effects of social experience, but concepts of existence are exposed to it, and the structure of political theories includes both. In an ontology consisting exclusively of concepts of being, individual bias could be cancelled out through verification, but such a strictly "scientific" ontology would be unable to account for the experience of social existence and could not give rise therefore to an idea of society. There are few ostensive properties of man's being which could give an indication of his social life. The ostensive (i.e. physiological) properties of man refer merely to the organism of the individual, failing to account for his social relations beyond the sphere of the immediate family. Up to a certain point the social organization of a family checks with the ostensive properties of the organism, for neither the reproduction of the species, not the rearing of the young is possible in isolation. However, beyond the immediate family much of the complex of social relations remains enigmatic, when an empirical approach is taken to the definition of the concept of man. Political theories cannot be restricted to a purely empirical view, since they deal with society beyond the sphere of the individual and his family just as much, as they deal with the individual himself. Individualist theories may conceive of society as the coexistence of discrete individuals, but they must introduce some concept or idea to account for social relations in the sphere of economy, culture, politics and jurisdiction. Through the use of such heuristic concepts, even the most ardently scientific of individualist theories allows for the entry of historical-social influences into the thesis. Such an influence is necessarily derived from some aspect of the experience and knowledge of the collective life-order, for a person cannot be said to develop such concepts entirely by himself, but selects, adopts, or at the most transforms, the concepts already present in his milieu. Hence both the heuristic concept's content and its form will be influenced by his environment. Using such a concept in conjunction with an empirical ontology of being, the thinker's ontology of existence enters into the theory (though in a secondary form) in that the objectified meanings derived from the integral view of man follow through the utilization of a set of concepts whose content as well as form have been influenced by the thinker's social existence. Thus existential influence is present even when the basic content of the theory is objective.

Now, *collectivist* theories are exposed to this, as well as to other factors of influence from the thinker's milieu, not only as regards the selection of their heuristic concepts and method, but also with respect to the basic *content* of the theory. Since collectivist theories are built upon a concept of man as a social entity, the thinker's experience of existence will be directly reflected in the content of his thought. The heuristic concepts are utilized to adapt this existential content for the evaluation of being, and thus to subordinate the individual aspect of man (and objects in general) to their collective, interrelated aspect. As a result collectivist theories are fully exposed to historical-social influences, while individualist thought can be analysed to an objective base, impervious to existential influence, and to a superstructure of theoretical concepts subject to it. Now we have said that the heuristic concepts of contemporary political theories represent the hypostatization of the thinker's already existent idea of reality. Thus to understand political theories, we must inquire into the orientation of the thinker's general ontology and find the pattern of influence shaping and moulding it.

The idea each man entertains of society manifests a modal polarity, since every civilized man incorporates in his person the synthesis of a "being" in the individual sense, and an "existence" in the social context. The thinking of all men can be analysed to this polarity, present in the structure of their knowledge as an ontology of being and an ontology of existence. The general orientation of the person depends upon the relative importance he attaches to one or the other of these ontologies. Whichever predominates in his thinking has much to do with the degree to which he exists as an individual, respectively as a social being. In general, individual being can be identified with the private life, and social existence with the public function of the person.[1] The limits of the two intermingle, however, and also exceed the above spheres. A person without public function still exists as a social entity, for he relates to others in his society – if not through supplying some service or product, then as its consumer. A fully isolated person could only be a lonely Robinson Crusoe, on an uninhabited part of the globe. On the other hand public functions do not necessarily bring persons into direct contact with others and make them by that token into social entities. A scientist working professionally at the research of a specific aspect of nature does not come into direct contact with society through his work; whatever human contact is necessary, it is an accessory means to the purpose of his activity: the gaining of further knowledge of independently real objects and processes. Indirectly, however, even the most absorbed scientist is brought into the social network of relations through his work, since his work is his livelihood and hence his means of existing as a consumer. His researches may not deal with human existence, but the fact that he engages in a specific activity assigns a place to the scientist in the social order, and makes him thereby – though indirectly – into a social entity. Thus there can be no fully individual being in human society, entirely devoid of social aspects, fully abstracted from the network of relations ex-

---

[1] Social relations arising out of the private life of the individual (friendship, comradeship etc.) play a secondary role in the life of a society, and can be subsumed under the heading of private being, rather than under that of social existence.

isting within the group; just as there can be no purely social entity either, not having individuality as a discrete being. In an extreme case – let us say that of an ambitious businessman or an enthusiastic clubwoman – the importance of the individual reality of the person may be reduced to a minimum, yet no person can exist merely in a social any more than in an individual context: all men have an objective being, and moments at least, when they think of the world in objective, rather than in subjective terms. Regardless how much a person usually comprehends his environment in terms of independently real objects (as typified by a scientist) or else as relationally real objects (typified by businessmen, socialites, etc.) the converse mode of comprehension will also be present in his thinking. In daily life some objects are regularly viewed in the context of existential relevance (food, for example) while others are usually understood as independently real (as the stars on a clear night).[1] Since both modes of comprehension are present in the idea of society of all civilized persons, no thinker attempting to attain a full understanding of man can avoid the inclusion of objective as well as subjective concepts in his theory. The question then remains *which* type of ontological concepts predominate in the thinker's idea of society, for the dominant ontology serves as the basis for the development or selection of the heuristic concepts through which the opposite ontology will be reinterpreted. Having added such concepts, the thinker can proceed by an analytic method: he has attributed a property to man permitting the comprehension of his being as well as his existence. But regardless whether concepts of existence serve as the base, or as the superstructure of his theory, the influences of the thinker's social existence are present in his thesis. The trained mind explicates further, but does not transcend the ideas of his societal time and place. The basis of his idea of society, if it is an ontology of being, may be free from influence of a historical origin, but the concepts with which it is expressed, and by means of which existence is interpreted, are subject to the conditioning effect of a historical society. The mode of speech and the mode of thought attributed to any single individual is not created by him; he finds at his disposal the language and the thought-pattern of his group. The given patterns of speech and thought may not only determine the avenue to compre-

---

[1] It is worthy of attention that children as well as primitive tribes comprehend objects as existing *for* them with the aid of heuristic concepts adopted to interpret the problematic of being in the light of their ontology of existence. Fairytales and the creatures of fantasy for children, myth and magic for primitives represent the child's and the primitive's subjectively oriented idea of reality.

sion open and accessible to him, but also make him continue using the angle and context in which objects and relations have hitherto been comprehended. In a final analysis the actual person does not create the concepts of his comprehensions, but continues the pattern developed before him by an endless series of responses to certain situations occurring more frequently, or having greater emphasis attributed to them in that social group, than elsewhere, and thus characterizing the society's position and reinforcing whatever tendencies to an interdetermined social existence have already been present[1]. Thus every person's political thought is doubly influenced by historical-social factors: on the one hand he finds situations typifying life in his historically interdetermined group, needing to be comprehended and efficiently dealt with, and on the other he has ready-made patterns of thought at his disposal, applied by his fellow beings to the presented societal situations. The influence of historical-social factors is reflected in both the basic ontological content, and the selection or development, of heuristicially functioning concepts in *collectivist* theories, while in *individualist* theories the ontological basic content may be free from such influence, but the theoretical superstructure will manifest it.

The sphere of a historically interdetermined existential pattern of life delimits the validity of political theories to the type of historical-social conditions which gave rise to them. However, even within that limitation a particular theory may not apply as a representative spokesman of the majority. We must consider that a stratified society can afford any one of a hierarchy of social standpoints. Each social standpoint (i.e. *class*) provides a typical level of existential satisfactions, and has a typical pattern of thought for expressing it. Consider, then, that the idea of society represents the individual's conception of the true nature of society. This is not necessarily a utopian idea, since the individual may equate his actual experience of society with his idea of it. This is the case in an extreme conservative point of view. But such a viewpoint is the exception rather than the rule, for the rule is a marked difference between what the individual holds that society is *essentially*, and what he finds it is *actually*. The completely conservative (exceptional) view supports the existing order without qualification, while the utopian picture of society moulds it concordantly with the hiatus between the idea, and the experienced reality of society. As agent of change, the idea of society can give rise to radical action (revolutions are motivated by a sharp differentiation between the idea

---

[1] cf. Karl Mannheim, *Ideology and Utopia*, and the theory of the Sociology of Knowledge school.

of society and the person's experience of social reality) or to a milder form of reformism. Conservatism, reformism, radicalism, are all based on the individual's idea of society, and its correspondence to his experience; a correspondence which is determined by the person's *class*. The revolutionary class represents a socio-economic standpoint which is wholly dissatisfactory, and the conservative class one which is fully satisfactory. Between the two we find various shades of reformism. The political thinking of the person is also conditioned by his social standpoint in that certain modes of comprehension and specific intellectual levels are typical for classes. To give an example: a manual labourer sees his society from the angle of relations which characterize his position. Above and beyond cognizing his own existence, he is conscious of his society and realizes (to a greater or lesser degree) the nature of the social order in which he lives. He formulates his political thought according to his deductions from his own end of the social relations. He does this with the concepts available to him, which in turn are the products of patterns of thought evolved in the history of his class. Being a manual labourer, he is likely to acquire an idea of reality consisting more of existential concepts than of concepts of being; he comprehends his environment mostly in the context of his own requirements. Consequently in his political thinking objective concepts will be subjected to the domination of his ontology of existence. He will thus formulate views which refer to society as seen from his viewpoint and pass judgment on his social order according to the *satisfactoriness* of his experiences. Depending on the degree of his satisfaction, he will profess conservative, reformist, or revolutionary convictions. Revolutionary, as well as conservative and reformist views may be expressed by various concepts. The thesis is that, as a general rule, history conditions the selection of the concepts, while social experience tends to be the main determinant of the judgment.

Now an intellectual, as well as a labourer, formulates his political theory by judgments and concepts derived from existential experience. An intellectual, however, may have a highly developed ontology of being in the structure of his idea of reality; he has the patterns of thought at his disposal in his milieu. He may then adopt either his existential concepts to fit his ontology of being, or *vice versa*. In either event his judgment will be conservative in spirit if his existential experience has been satisfactory, and reformist or revolutionary if he finds his existence unsatisfactory. Thus he can arrive at the same judgment as the manual labourer although he may use entirely different concepts and methods. Social factors have influenced the de-

velopment of his intellectual level and have thereby determined his
selection of the concepts as well. A satisfied individual, particularly if
he is an intellectual, is likely to acquire a general ontology wherein
concepts of being predominate, and, making use of heuristic concepts
suited to his level of intellect, may select those particular concepts
which correspond to his judgment of society – a judgment deriving
from the view afforded by a specific social standpoint. Dissatisfied
members of all classes are likely to turn to existentially charged concepts
and pronounce the same type of judgment on society, although they
do so by means of different patterns of thought. Class, as the relatively
similar existential standpoint of several persons, not only influences the
predominance of objective or subjective modes of thinking, but it tends
to determine the judgment an individual passes on his society. As no
person can experience relations other than those in his own society,
nor can use thought processes and concepts other than ones at his disposal, political theories do not transcend the limits of historical society,
but take position *within* it. When similarities in judgment obtain
between individuals of the same class but in different societies, these
judgments have nevertheless a *different* content, and are based on the
patterns of thought prevailing in that specific historical-social locus.

Political theories can, but do not necessarily manifest the influence
of a specific viewpoint. Since the opposite pole of a relationship can
be deduced from direct experience, and from that pole further relations can be inferred, the thinker has the full range of a society
within his scope of vision; he can deal with the range allowed him by
the sphere of interdetermination wherein he lives. He cannot transcend it, however, unless his actual existence exceeds the limits of the
society. The thinker includes that range of human relations into his
theory which he deduces from his experiences, hence the range of his
thinking does not exceed the sphere (or spheres) of interdetermination
in which he lives and through which he exists.

Unilateral judgments passed on society signify an identification
with the views of one class, and the disregard of the others. Only one
standpoint within society permits the formulation of a unilateral
judgment; more than one standpoint can come up merely with a
composite view. An intellectual when passing judgment on his society,
does not necessarily do so from his own social standpoint. In contra-
distinction to a labourer, who has little opportunity to deduce the
existential standpoint of others from his relations with them, an
intellectual has the opportunity of doing so and can, as a consequence,

adopt the viewpoint of any class he wishes. The adoption of a single viewpoint is expressed by a correspondingly clear-cut unilateral judgment. Such judgment signifies the restriction of the theory to the examination of a particular aspect of society, that aspect namely, which is directly evident from the class view-point adopted by the thinker. Theories passing unilateral judgments refer to their society, and have as their content the common social experience of all people in that society. By virtue of a judgment which is that of one class, rather than of all classes, such a theory is restricted to dealing with one aspect of the common content; society is pronounced to be good or bad, progressive or reactionary, or any shade between these extremes, not, however, a composite of the judgments actually pronounced by the different classes of people. Insofar as a thinker allies himself with a class of a different intellectual level, he expresses the content of their thoughts, pronounces their judgments, but does so by different concepts, and through the use of different thought processes than the typical members of that class. Although political theories are not necessarily allied to the thought of one group, but may cover the entire range of a historical society, all thinkers are exposed first of all to the influence of their own social standpoint, and then to the influence of the standpoint of their sympathies. These influences act on the thinkers by lending them the optic of their own or that of another class. Political theories which are expressly conservative, revolutionary, or which adopt one specific set of criteria for reforms, can be analysed to an influence originating from the allegiance of the thinker with the social position of one particular group.

Conservative, reformist and revolutionary philosophies advocated in different societies have only their judgment of society in common. They refer to different spheres of experience and have different contents; they utilize the thought-patterns and concepts available to them, and hence even formulate their judgments differently. Collectivist theories, based upon an ontology of existence, are liable to the influence of historical-social factors as regards their basic content and theoretical superstructure. Individualist theories, founded on the constant, ostensive properties of man and nature, are subject to historical-social influence insofar as they must of necessity make use of heuristic concepts to investigate and interpret social experience. As a result, no political theory can escape from the conditioning effect of a specific social setting, although the setting affects different theories to various degrees, corresponding to whether concepts of being or concepts of existence predominate in the thinker's idea of society.

THE INFLUENCE OF
THEORETICAL AND INSTITUTIONALIZED
PRINCIPLES ON POPULAR POLITICAL THOUGHT

Every man, we have found, has a general idea of reality including two kinds of ontological concepts: concepts of being, deriving from abstracted comprehension of objects, and concepts of existence, following through relational comprehensions. The concept of man includes a combination of the two categories of concepts, a combination which gives primacy either to one, or to the other of the categories. The question of primacy is largely, but not fully, determined by the general orientation of the subjects's idea of general reality. An integral ontology oriented toward concepts of existence may yet tolerate a concept of man wherein individual being is primary and social existence secondary, notwithstanding the inconsistency obtaining between the resulting idea of society and the idea of general reality. Conversely, a person oriented toward the abstracted, objective comprehension of reality in general, may formulate a concept of man wherein social existence predominates, and individual being is subordinate. The reason for the tolerance of such discrepancies lies with the loose, a-logical construction of most personal ontologies. Such outlooks do not signify a thoroughly systematized, logically developed, fully consistent view of all of reality, but manifest discords which could come to light only in a thorough analysis – which, however, in most cases is never undertaken. As a consequence it is quite possible that a person, such as a scientist, for example, should approach his own area of investigation objectively, and treat social problems subjectively, just as a publicist may regard the sphere of society in terms of mutual human interest and yet be ready to abstract his thinking from the context of requirement and fulfilment when dealing with nature. It is the rule rather than the exception that environmental objects in frequent pragmatic contact with persons are treated as relationally real, in the context of their function for the subject's existence, while objects that are more removed from such pragmatic relations are comprehended as independently real, in abstraction from the subject's existence. Only a fully systematized idea of reality could integrate both categories of concepts into an integral whole. To do so, it must introduce theoretical concepts for the heuristic function of interpreting one category in terms of the other. Such is the case with political theories.

Now, political thought has been defined here as being centred on the individual's idea of society. This idea derives from his concept of man. Political theory represents the systematization of this concept, by bringing it in harmony with a general conception of reality. We have outlined how historical-social influences act on this system-atization-process, and serve to interpret reality concordantly with the individual's social experience. In this process particular political theories emerge. Those that are institutionalized become active social agents, and shape popular political thought. Since most people do not systematize their ontological *Weltanschauung*, an institutionalized theory may shape the individual's concept of man, without bringing it into conflict with the more stable elements of his general outlook. Thus it may come about that a political theory based on a firmly committed ontological standpoint may effect a transformation in the social outlook of a people, leaving their culture and national heritage intact. This discussion is devoted to the exploration of the possible effects various theoretical and institutionalized political theories may have upon popular political thought.

The Ontological Principle of Social Organization

Political theories provide effective bases for social action. All lines of policy evidence the ontological structure of a theory, for every active policy is based either on the primal consideration of the individual or of the collectivity. Various shadings of individualism and collectivism exist, but the orientation of every political programme clearly testifies to the genus of the theory: the programme's point of departure is either the individual – his rights, his freedom, satisfaction, etc.; or the collectivity – the various collectively operated organizations and institutions that make up social existence. All programmes deal with the individual as with the collectivity, but individualism deduces the criteria of the collectivity from the well-being of the individual, while collectivism deduces criteria for the individual from the organization of the collectivity. The ethical accent lies on individual good in one, and on collective good in the other. The primary premiss of all political programmes is an ontological one (if not explicitly, then by implication) and this premiss gives rise to the theory's principle of organization. The principle of organization advocated by all political theories is an *ontological* principle giving primacy either to the individual or to the collectivity, according to whether individual being or social existence is considered determinant in the theory's concept of man. Monarchies, Aristocracies, Oligarchies, Dictatorships, Democracies, Socialism and Communism, in fact all constitutions and forms of government, can be analysed to a particular variant of an ontological principle. Communism is evidently built on a *specific* political theory. It is less evident (and is in fact often questioned) that individualist regimes can be analysed to a central principle. While we are ready to concede that liberal governments do not as a rule operate on the basis of one specific political theory, the fact that they are constitutional and put into effect a consistent programme corresponding to the structure of a society, permits their analysis to a central, institutionalized ontological principle. Insofar as a civilized society is organized, it is organized on some principle, and that principle can be explicated by deduction. All societies adopt an ontological principle, although in some that principle is explicit and *a priori*, in others implicit and can be explicated only *a posteriori*. A liberal society manifests an ontological principle also, even if it tolerates contradictions and gives seats in parliament to the opposition: for contradictions obtain only in thought, and not in practice. The contradiction of one political proposition by a member of the opposition is itself part of a structure in which that contradiction is present as the concept of the freedom of individual opinion. Contradictions cannot be put into practice; their effect on social organization signifies already their resolution. In the structure of a liberal society we do find oppositions, deriving from contradictory views, but the very fact that theoretical contradictions obtain is a characteristic feature of liberalism, and forms one of the premisses of its ontological principle. The contradiction of being is non-being, and that of existence is non-existence; the contradiction of society as a sphere of being and existence is a sphere of non-being and non-existence. What applies to the whole applies also to the part: every aspect or part of a society either is or is not, and if it is, it is either in one way or in another, but never both. *That* which is, and *how* it is, can nevertheless be the result of the clash of contradictory views. We maintain that the fact that a liberal society admits contradictions in its choice of policies, does not mean that its structure incorporates contradictions. The structure manifests only the *effects* of contradictions occurring on the level of thought. Although we cannot derive any one political theory from an analysis of the political thought of a liberal government, we *can* derive an ontological principle from the structure of liberal society. Deduction from the actual structure of any society whatsoever will yield a set of principles which are systematic and unitary insofar as they are interconnected in the social body. They are systematic and capable of being explicated as a central principle of social organization regardless whether they are founded on a systematic theory or on isolated and perhaps contradictory trains of thought. Every society is operated by an ontological principle and that principle exerts an influence on the development of political thought in the ranks of its members. The thought itself may be admitted into parliament, or excluded from it. Liberal statutes permit the institutionalization of popular political thought, while dogmatic statutes, based on a pre-determined and in itself systematic view of society, are reluctant to admit the people's thinking into the political programme. Nevertheless, popular political thought exercises an effective influence on the insti-tutionalized principle of all societies, regardless of its exclusion or inclusion in the political programme.

The ontological principle of social organization is based either ex-plicitly or implicitly on an integral concept of man: it takes into account the individual being as well as the social existence of each person. A minimum amount of objective understanding of man as a physical organism must be included in the principle, and a minimum of comprehension of the interrelations which determine the life of the person must be present as well. An operative ontological principle must view man both as an individual being in a world of objective givenness, and as a social existent in the human world of need and fulfilment. Hence an ontology of being must be brought into the con-text of the ontology of existence, or the ontology of existence into that of the ontology of being. Since being and existence are founded on different modes of comprehending the same environmental reality, the two ontologies cannot be directly explained in terms of each other. Either our objective concepts of being must be subjectively evaluated and re-comprehended as aspects of existence, or else our existential concepts must be analysed in the light of our ontology of being. Whichever mode of comprehension is understood in terms of the other determines whether the resulting principle of government is individu-alist or collectivist.

(i) *Theoretical Principles*

(A) HISTORY – The history of political theory is also the history of the evolution of the individualist and collectivist principle. In the following we shall sample some of the major theories and schools, and consider how they contributed to the development of these bifurcating principles.

The first thinker of antiquity to unequivocally commit himself to one of these principles, was Epicurus. His utilitarian materialism in politics rested on the acknowledgment of the primacy of individuals who, attempting to fulfil themselves, constitute the social body to assure their safe satisfaction. Not all political theories were so clearly committed, however.

The first and perhaps the most important works of political theory, those of Plato (*Politeia*) and Aristotle (*Politics*) were not. Still, Plato advocated a theory which is essentially individualistic, and accounts for society by attributing theoretical, heuristically functioning concepts to the being of man. Plato's heuristic concepts are contained in his view of the soul. The human soul, considered by him to be an immaterial agent, superior in nature to the body, and somewhat hindered by it in the performance of its higher functions, manifests a tripartite division: it consists of a rational, a spirited, and an acquisitive part. The rational part is the highest, and in the well-regulated man takes the leading role. The spirited element comes next, which provides the incentive for action, and is the seat of virtue and courage. The lowest part is the acquisitive one, which incorparates base instincts as well, and is to be brought under control by virtue and temperance, i.e. by the higher levels of the soul. This concept represents the attribution of a non-ostensive property to man, which permits Plato to develop a heuristic method with respect to the analysis of social existence. Plato conceives of three classes of men; in each class a different part of the soul predominates. Representing the rational part are the philosopher-kings, individuals who by nature and education, could subordinate their baser psychic elements to the rational part of the soul. The second class is constituted by the soldiers or guardians, a class whose souls have developed a remarkable spirited, war-like element, kept under control by virtue and courage. The third and lowest class is made up of acquisitive individuals, the workers of all kinds whose basic virtue is temperance. Now the fact that for the two upper classes Plato foresaw a form of community life wherein property was collective, and monogamous marriage abolished, must not be taken as proof of Plato's collectivism – this form of life was foreseen not only for a minority of the people (and was held to be a practical impossibility in the *Laws*), but the recommendation followed a hierarchy in social organization which was not a hierarchy of existence but one of *being:* which persons were to belong to a class was not determined by their social existence, but by their individual being; their being was seen to determine their social function. Hence the ontology of being predominates in the scheme, and serves as basis for the addition of a heuristic concept (the soul) by means of which the experience of social existence is interpreted and the social structure defined. Since Plato's idea of society transcended his social experience, the *Politeia* served as a model for subsequent *utopian* political theories.

When we consider Aristotle's *Politics* his conception of man as a political animal might, at first glance, lead to the conclusion that his idea of society was based on a predominantly subjective view of man (man as a relational entity). Better knowledge of Aristotelian thought soon shows the fallacy of such an assumption. For it becomes evident that when Aristotle expounds the importance of the political community as source and sustainer of typically human life, he arrives at the definition of the concept of man not through the consideration of social existence, but of being: Aristotle attributed the concepts of form (as the coincidence of the formal, efficient and final causes) and matter (the material cause) to the being of all entities. It is this union which makes every object the determinate kind of thing it is. All being (including man) is determined in Aristotle's view more by inherent principles, than by the interaction of formed entities. While the latter view could lead to the conclusion that the totality of existent entities determines each particular (and thus in society the collectivity could be seen to determine the individual), this view has not been endorsed by Aristotle. For him man is what he is primarily through the entelechy of his intrinsic being, rather than through external determination by relational (social) existence. Correspondingly for Aristotle the highest good for man lies in theoretical inquiry and the search for truth, and not in political life or in any form of practical activity.

Following the rise of the Christian era, new theoretical concepts were attributed to man's being. The basic idea of a hierarchy of being was set forth in Christian thought by attributing the highest level of being to God. As a result, early Christianity took a rather negative attitude toward earthy society, (St. Augustine's *De Civitate Dei*) declaring it to be *civitas diaboli*, a state of the devil. The theoretical concept of soul was still attributed to man, and his being analysed by means of this heuristic method. The importance of earthly existence was subordinated to the value of living in accordance with man's eternal soul; man is to be guided by his own essentially Godlike being, and to aspire to admittance to a higher sphere of being after death. Consequently earthly authority was considered secondary, and the rights of royal power themselves seen as of popular, human origin, and to be abolished if abused (Thomas Aquinas). The decline of Christian influence in civic affairs left subsequent political thought with a hierarchy of being without a supernatural figurehead. The first class of being was attributed to kings, and the level of being scaled from the Monarch down through the nobility to the common man. As over the centuries the latter advanced to higher economic and intellectual levels, the popular idea of society began to envisage the being of all men as equal. With that began the long series of demands for equal rights. The theory of popular rights has been advocated by the "Monarchomachi" (such, as Beza, Hotman, Danaeus, etc.) most of them using a form of the social covenant theory. The idea of this original contract, finding full expression in the works of Roger Williams and John Locke, was built on the assumption of the essential equality of all men: equal individuals joined together, and by mutual consent formed a state and placed fiduciary trust in the supreme power. Its most ardent defender was Rousseau, in whose thoughts the sovereignity of the people took on an even more democratic aspect, since he saw each individual as having a share in the moulding of the "general will" which, in the last count, determines the structure and order of society.

The 19th century witnessed a turning in the evolution of political theories in the West. For much of Europe that century was undoubtedly a period of crisis, brought about by the incompatibility of rapid industrialization and a still feudal social structure. Under the pressure of increasingly problematic conditions, political thought went to extremes. While adherents of the "social covenant" explanation of society levelled the concept of man for all classes ("all men are born equal") and adopted a viewpoint generally associated with Democracy, an opposing school of political thinkers developed the collectivist principle. Following up Aristotelian implications of society as a natural, organic unity, organicist theories were already proposed by Vitoria, Hobbes, and later, Spencer. Prompted by patriotism and the monistic tendencies of 19th century German idealism, and no doubt aided by the deterministic arguments of such thinkers as Spinosa, Fichte and La Mettrie, organicist naturalism transformed into full collective determinism, finding clear expression in Hegel's philosophy of history. Not only did Hegel treat the individual as the embodiment of an Idea, but he also reversed the individualist ontological principle of social organization: he considered the individual to be determined by the collectivity, to be essentially nothing more than a dialectical moment in the social process. Hegelian dialectics proved to be a suitable principle for expressing inherently collectivist tendencies in the excessively stratified, and on the whiole dissatisfactory social order of 19th century European society. The socialistically oriented intellectuals of that time, under the leadership of Marx and Engels, found in dialectics the cosmological buttress for their social, political, and moral convictions. By applying dialectics as a method of inquiry and as a principle of social process, and by substituting realistic materialism in place of Hegelian idealism, they found the theoretical framework for the conceptualization of a subjective view of society, treating all aspects of social life from the viewpoint of "practice," in the sense of human-sensuous activity (Marx). At the same time the adoption of the dialectical principle led to the consideration of the essence, characteristics and personality of the individual as socially determined. Thought, spirit, was found to be a reflection of an objective dialectical process wherein the individual is part of opposing poles (the thesis and antithesis of the class-struggle), and his thinking, behaviour, his individuality in short, determined by his social (class) position.

A collectivist concept of man has been inherent in the thought of the pre- and non-Marxian socialists as well (e.g. Owen, St. Simon, Fourier, etc.). It is the accomplishment of Marx and Engels, however, to substantiate this collectivist concept by an integral cosmological scheme, comprising an interpretation of social processes (historical materialism) and an interpretation of general reality (dialectical materialism). Their basic achievement (whether it is positively or negatively judged) lies, in the opinion of this writer, in having developed an essentially subjective approach to the problem of reality (one, that is, wherein concepts of existence serve as the foundation for a heuristic concept serving to interpret concepts of being) into a sociological scheme, and then having applied the principal categories and method of that scheme to evolve a cosmological scheme. Leaving the detailed analysis of this theory to a subsequent chapter, we shall merely note here that we subsume all varieties of Socialism, "utopian," as well as "scientific," in the category of *collectivism*.

(B) APPLICATIONS – Individualism and collectivism in the history of political theory, derive from the personal experiences of the thinkers. As notwithstanding divergences, the *bases* of experience in all epochs are universally human, the ultimate implications of these two categories of political theories are by no means essentially contradictory, nor even opposing. As a matter of fact both could attain the ideal form of society, one as the ideal of being, the other as that of existence. We need only to consider that an idea of society which is thoroughly existentialized through the addition of a heuristic concept corresponding to the ontology of existence and institutionalized as the organizational principle of a society, is based on the comprehension of man's environmental experiences in the context of his requirements. A correct evaluation of all objects through the understanding of their relation to the factors of human existence could produce an organization of social life wherein all objects find the relation to every person which best suits his own *existential* needs. On the other hand an understanding of the external world by virtue of its empirical properties, and the addition then of a heuristic concept for the understanding of the social world of humanity as a logical resultant, or part of, the objective world, could place man into that relation with the environment which best suits his *being*.

Now individual being and social existence are two aspects of man's actual givenness, approached by two different modes of comprehending it. A social organization based on the full and correct evaluation of man's objective being would satisfy all requirements of his existence, while the purposeful and rational fulfilment of all his existential requirements would afford his optimum being. A political theory based on the full and correct knowledge of the individual would just as surely satisfy the social animal as the theory based on the full knowledge of social requirements would fulfill the individual. Inasmuch as full, verifiable knowledge of either man's being or existence is not possible, the difference between the individual and collective idea lies mainly in the area of compromise. Liberals wish to make sure of knowing the individual first, and hold social organization to be subject to the progress of their knowledge of the factors of being. Socialists search for an understanding of the pattern of existential requirements, and hold that knowledge of the individual becomes clarified only in the context of a knowledge of society. Hence liberals are willing to fit social organization to suit individual being, while socialists wish to suit individual being to social existence. Since neither do liberals fully know all aspects of being, nor are socialists conversant with all aspects of existence, both categories of political theories proceed on the hypothesis that whatever knowledge they have of man's givenness is sufficient to bring about a clarification of the still unknown aspects. As a result the insufficient knowledge of being brings with it a certain lack of organization by liberals, and insufficient knowledge of existence involves the disregard of the individual by socialists. Thereby man's existential requirements are relatively shortchanged in liberal theories, and his individual rights underestimated in socialist doctrines.

At the actual stage of knowledge liberals and socialists are at odds and see their direct adversaries in each other, notwithstanding the potential coincidence of their postulates, given a full and correct knowledge of the respective premises. The method of interpreting man's existence in the light of his being gives very different results still, from that derived from an interpretation of his being in terms of an idea of existence. Accordingly an orientation toward the individual does not coincide with the orientation toward collective life, and the ideas of liberals differ sharply from those of the socialists.

Unlike non-ideological socialism, Marxist Communism proceeds to build a social structure by institutionalizing a theory which claims to know man fully, to know both his being (organism, consciousness, spirit) and his existence (the correlation of the social modes of production with the forces of production, determining human existence). Thus while liberals and non-Marxist socialists tend to be non-evaluative, basing actual policies on the minimum number of theoretical assumptions (although the ontological principle of individualism or collectivism is always present, regardless whether its presence is acknowledged or not), Marxism dogmatizes a theoretical view of man as absolute and unconditional truth, and claims to have discovered the "objective laws of social processes." Hence Communism sees its direct adversaries in both liberals and in non-Marxist socialists, condemning the former for a fallacious view of social reality, and the latter for its hesitation to accept the Marxian explanation of the adopted ontological principle. Although noninstitutionalized political thought may eventually approach a middle road by profiting from an exchange of experiences under various social climates, *rapprochement* on the institutionalized level could take place only when dogmatism is removed from the constitutional structure of all societies.

(ii) Institutionalized Principles

(A) HISTORY – Every historical body of political thought, we maintain, has a basic ontological content which has been officially adopted as
the central principle of the social order. The various institutions designed
to maintain and develop that order reflect the basic principle in their
structure. As each organized society operates by virtue of the various
institutions of public order, and all its institutions reflect the basic
idea of an ontological principle, constituted states are built on, and
function to conserve, a particular view of the relation of the individual
to the collectivity. If this relation is seen to be determined more by the
individual than by society as a whole, the ontological principle of the
constituted state is individualist; in the opposite event it is collectivist.
As there are great differences in the forms of constituted states, and
insofar as each specific form is associated by either an individualist
or a collectivist principle of social organization, we may subsume the
major varieties of constituted states according to the principle they
serve to institutionalize.

The Individualist States

Individualist states are built on the comprehension of man as a
discrete being. They regard the individual as essentially selfdetermined,
and define him by his ostensive properties. Individualist states tend
to follow the guidance of individual (as opposed to mass) psychology,
to take into account modern western-type sociology basing its studies
on the socially relevant characteristics of the individual, and to adopt
a view of history wherein major events are traced to the interaction
of personalities in leading positions. Since social phenomena cannot all
be directly accounted for by a study of the ostensive characteristics of
the individual, heuristically functioning theoretical concepts are
implicit in the operations of individualist states. Implicit, though
seldom explicit (since individualist states do not, as a rule, embrace
one specific theory officially) is the concept of human *will*, prompting
individuals to seek social relations for improving their mode of existence
through a division of labour in production, enjoyment of culture, play
and selfdefense. Voluntarism does not imply that individuals are determined by their social relations. Implicit in the argument is always the
assumption that the relations are determined by the interaction of the
characteristics of the given individuals. Hence the individual is seen
to determine the structure of the collectivity: the sum total of individuals in a given nation determines the constitution of its form of state.

Built on this ontological principle are Monarchies, Autocracies, Oligarchies on the one hand, and Republics and Federations of a democratic content on the other. As we shall discuss, the principle of individualism may be subdivided into two categories, of which the first applies to Monarchies, Autocracies and Oligarchies, as the *Aristocratic* category of individualism, and the second to democratic Republics and Federations as individualism's *Democratic* category.

The former forms of states may be subsumed under the common term "Aristocracy," since regardless whether one man rules or a group dominates, society is divided into an aristocratic and a common faction. In this respect it makes no difference whether the rights of the aristocracy are hereditary or have been obtained by individual initiative. In both events the ruling faction dominates by virtue of a status which elevates him above the common folk, and lends to his being a distinguishing feature. The Aristocrat (whether a King, an Autocrat, or a member of the Oligarchy) has certain rights with respect to the totality; he relates *to*, but is not a *part* of, that totality. This basic political thought finds expression in the person of an Autocrat: he incorporates full individual being in his person. The Autocrat is not a part of the collectivity, he is above it, he *rules* over it. There is a caste-hierarchy in the aristocratic state ranging from members of the aristocracy (the nobility in Monarchies, and members of the sole political party in Dictatorships) to the middle classes, down to the common folk. The caste-system of Aristocracy represents a hierarchy of *being*, where each person is an individual, but exists in one of a set of qualitatively distinct levels. The complete, full individual, with all rights of individual being is the highest aristocrat, the Autocrat alone. Thereafter come various levels of being, reaching ultimately to the landless peasant and the wage labourer, whose beings are subordinate, and whose rights are correspondingly restricted. Each level, starting from the Autocrat and reaching to the common folk, is subordinate to the higher, without ever entering into the conception of its principal. In Aristocracies we have a series of distinct, superimposed levels of being, and not one totality of which all persons are parts. Hence the general content of the political programme of Aristocracies is individualist, rather than collectivist. This basic content is the product of the society's history. Aristocratic forms of state gave expression to a wide-spread, generally accepted view of society, according to which different classes of people are not merely socially, but intrinsically different: a nobleman, for example, incorporates a higher level of being than a peasant, even if the peasant should have amassed greater wealth, and thus could assure an easier existence for himself. The constituted state giving formal, institutional expression to this notion exercises a conservative influence on the evolution of political thought, tending to preserve the belief in the intrinsic superiority of the ruling classes. Nevertheless, political thought is dynamic, open to manifold influences, of which better education, more extensive social contacts and greater freedom of movement and expression contribute particularly to the erosion of the notion of the hierarchy of being. As Aristocracies are built on this notion, and cannot abandon it without causing the downfall of the constitutional system as a whole, an increasing tension obtains between the institutionalized, and the popular idea of society. Eventually the point is reached when the stratification of the social system, based as it is on qualitative differences among individuals, becomes untenable in the eyes of the majority.

Reform then takes place through choosing one of two alternatives: (a) keeping the ontological principle of individualism, and dissociating social stratification from the essential hierarchy of being, or (b) discarding the individualist principle, and adopting the collectivist one in its place. The former alternative requires a series of reforms which may gradually transform the system, without first overthrowing the regime, while the latter calls for a *coup* which usually involves violence and a full blown revolt.

We shall consider Democracy next, as the principle of social organization capable of reforming the ills of Aristocracy through parliamentary measures. Democratic regimes can be subdivided into two constituted forms of state: Monarchy of a democratic content (where the aristocratic constitution is merely symbolic) and Republic. Constitutional Monarchy removes the inversion of individual being and gives each person equal rights, the person of the Monarch being conceived merely as symbolic, rather than representative of the power and authority of an aristocracy. (Constitutional Monarchies [e.g. The Netherlands, England, and Scandinavian countries] have representative government, just as the Democratic Republics [France, USA, Federal Germany, etc.] have). The characteristic of Democracy is the attribution of full individual rights to each person, the consideration of everyone as a discrete, free being, and the conception of the government's function as serving (rather than ruling) the people. While each person has a public function, he does not exhaust his personality in that function, but keeps his own being above and beyond his socially relevant activity.

The highest personage (the President of the Republic and the Prime Minister of the head of State) has a public function which consists of *serving* the common good just as every other person. The person is always seen behind the function, and the individual's basic rights are those of the person and not of the office temporarily occupied by him. Only the Monarch, (in constitutional Monarchies) keeps a higher level of individuality, but merely as a symbol of the continued solidarity of all people of the nation. Since constitutional Monarchies and Democratic Republics do no more than re-invert the hierarchy of being obtaining in an Aristocracy making the State serve society, rather than society serve the State, they do not *change* the basic content of political thought. Democracies are still built on the conception of man as individual, but attribute to each person full individual being and corresponding rights. The State as such is not incorporated in any person, it consists only of offices which actual persons occupy, elected by others for this function. In the re-inverted hierarchy of Democracy the office serves the people; every office is occupied by a person, all people have equal constitutional rights, and the State – the offices – remain functions to be assumed by persons elected for a specific time. Thus a hierarchy of offices results, filled by essentially equal beings.

The fundamental difference between Aristocracies and Democracies lies in this: Aristocratic societies are stratified because the being of each man is seen to determine his existence, and *essential* differences are held to obtain between the being of different individuals. In Democratic societies, however, the being of all individuals, although still prior to their social existence, is considered to be essentially equal; differences in the level of existence of different men are ascribed to *accidental* differences of their being (better education, professional training, etc.).

The idea of society formed by the emancipated masses of advanced societies demands equalization, and Democracies equalized the social structures of Aristocracies by removing all *essential* differences from the concept of the people. Democracies know only *accidental* differences qualifying equal citizens for different functions and thus permitting a stratified system based on equal individual rights. The ontological principle has not changed; it is still that of individualism. But the individualist concept of man has been equalized, so that the idea of society is now Democratic-Individualist, rather than Aristocratic-Individualist.

The Collectivist States

Equalization of the Aristocratic regime's hierarchy of being can also be attained by discarding the individualist view of society, and adopting the collectivist conception in its place. The collectivist principle regards the individuality of man as a product of his society. Society as a whole is seen as a primal entity, of which individuals are component parts. As the function of the part becomes meaningful only when the character of the totality is known, so can the individual be understood only in the context of the structure and nature of his society. Such a view can be traced back to the predominance of an ontology of existence, evaluating social reality in terms of need and its fulfilment through social relations. The collectivist principle of social organization gives rise to constituted forms of state which rely in their operations on mass psychology, and on a form of sociology derived from, and subordinated to a specific holistic view of history, wherein not individuals, but social and culture-groups are the motive forces. Finally collectivist states have shown a tendency to explicate their ontological principle by defining a particular set of heuristically functioning theoretical concepts serving to reinterpret concepts of being in the light of a dominant ontology of existence. There have been two, more or less explicit theories institutionalized by constituted states in the 20th century. One was Fascism, and the other is Communism. Fascism is the less explicit of the two. Its greatest shortcoming appears to consist in its failure to develop a rational heuristic concept for the interpretation of individual human being as a function of collective existence. The theoretical concept of Fascism falls short of being rationally satisfactory in two respects: *one,* it is vague and tends to become mystical in use; *two,* it has a limited applicability. This concept is the "Herrenvolk" a form of racism the essence of which found clearest expression in Alfred Rosenberg's definition of the "race-soul." This soul is apparently an attribute of the collectivity rather than of the individual, and thus requires the subordination of individual peculiarities to the conformity standards of racial attributes. While it thus foresees the domination of the collectivity over the individual within the confines of the race, it makes no definite assertions concerning the ontological principle of organization applicable to people who do not possess this common soul (as the Slavs, for example).

The delimited applicability of the Fascist concept is expressed by Hitler in *Mein Kampf*

For myself and for all true National Socialists there exists only one doctrine: nation and fatherland. What we have to fight for is to make secure the existence and the expansion of our race and of our nation, to rear its children and to keep pure the blood, the freedom and the independence of the fatherland, so that our nation may get ripe for the mission which the creator of this universe has assigned to it." [1]

Collectivism within the chosen nation and race is of an extreme variety. Mussolini writes in *La Dottrina del Fascismo*

Everything is in the State, and nothing human or spiritual exists, much less has value, outside the State... Outside the State there can be neither individuals nor groups... Fascism is a religious conception in which man is seen in his immediate relationship with a superior law and with an objective will that transcends the particular individual and raises him to conscious membership of a spiritual society... The man of Fascism is an individual who is nation and fatherland... [2]

Owing to its confused and mystical heuristic concept the Fascist doctrine could never exceed the bounds of the veneration of the "Herrenvolk" and of Mussolini's "Etatismo." Its collectivism was limited to these areas, and whatever latent potentials collectivist ideas may have had elsewhere, they could not be inflamed by Fascism, except by a stretch of the race concept surpassing the bounds of what most people could accept as rational.

The collectivism of Communism differs from that of Fascism precisely in having developed a universally applicable theoretical concept: the dialectics of material evolution applying to every society as well as to all nature. Owing to the universality of the Communist idea of collectivist society Communism differs from Fascism in its proclaimed purposes and its real potency. Communists seek to establish the world domination of the proletariat, while Fascists were determined to bring to power a particular nation or people, or, in the case of the Italian Fascists, to predominate in a specific region. Supported by their rationalized heuristic concept, Communists can claim to have the key to the objective evaluation of social and historical processes. They can thus advertise a "scientific" rule, as opposed to the reliance on intuitions by the National Socialist leaders. The Party is omnipotent in both systems, but in Communism the Party organization is international and its programme is held to be universal and unconditionally valid for all people, while the Nazi Party's organization and programme

---

[1] Adolf Hitler, *Mein Kampf*, München, 1925–27, p. 234.
[2] from B. Mussolini, *La Dottrina del Fascismo*, 1934.

was strictly delimited to the privileged nations and races. Fascism appears to be of the past. Communism, on the other hand, is very much a part of the present, and looms as a major force of the future as well. Consequently under contemporary constituted states incorporating the principle of collectivism we must understand primarily the states of the Socialist bloc. A possible exception is given by Israel, where a form of collectivism was initiated, but is now on the decline.[1] Elsewhere whatever spontaneous tendencies for collectivism may be given, are immediately exploited by Communists, with the result that if and when collectivism becomes institutionalized the constituted state is apt to be patterned on the Marxist-Leninist blueprint. We may thus discuss collectivist states as typified by the nations of the Communist bloc.

Communist society is envisaged to arise in the USSR in about twenty years. The present is considered a transitory phase from Capitalism to Communism for the entire Communist bloc. Under that interpretation the nations of the bloc are allowed extra specifics which do not characterize either Capitalism or the final form of Communism. The major specific is the "Dictatorship of the Proletariat." It is by virtue of referring most undesiderata obtaining in the Communist regime to the exigencies of this transitory phase that the salient discrepancies between the idea of Communist society and the social reality of contemporary Communist states are explained away. There is a striking parallel in the schism of theory and practice between Fascism and Communism. Both entertained a chiliastically utopian idea of society (their ideal of society was removed from actual reality and involved a prognostic of the future), and both made constant calls for collective heroism, transforming thereby the national atmosphere into a state of permanent revolution. The closing of the schism between utopia and reality was foreseen by both doctrines to take place through a collective effort wherein the subordination of individual interests to the common good transforms into the long-range good of the individual. As, however, even the most attractive vision of the future loses much of its power to provide incentive for action when action results in the sacrifice of the individual's immediate

---

[1] Israel's collectivism derived most likely from the loyality ties of the Jewish people developed during the centuries of effort spent in surviving as a particular race and culture on foreign soil, in face of persecution and intolerance. The danger and difficulties accompanying the birth of Israel tended to bring these ties into sharp focus, aided also by the fulfilment of a biblical utopia. The result was the submerging of individual values under the weighty problems of the collectivity. It is significant, however, that as soon as conditions began to stabilize, individualism reasserted itself, taking the form of a liberal democracy.

interests for a future blessing, Fascism, like Communism made use of a totalitarian dictatorship to effectuate its programme, and coupled it with a full scale propaganda effort. In fact these two regimes represent a novel form of state in history: the totalitarian dictatorship. Friedrich and Brzezinski contend that "totalitarian dictatorship is historically unique and *sui generis*. It is also our conclusion from all the facts available to us that fascist and communist totalitarian dictatorships are basically alike, or at any rate more nearly like each other than like any other system of government, including earlier forms of autocracy."[1]

The above authors define the basic features of totalitarian dictatorship as consisting of (i) *An official ideology* (a doctrine covering all vital aspects of man's existence to which everyone living in that society is supposed to adhere, at least passively; this ideology is characteristically focused and projected toward a perfect final state of mankind, that is to say, it contains a chiliastic claim, based upon a radical rejection of the existing society and conquest of the world for the new one); (ii) *a single party typically led by one man, the "dictator"* (consisting of a relatively small percentage of the population, who are unquestioningly dedicated to the ideology and are prepared to assist in every way in promoting its general acceptance, such a party being hierarchically, oligarchically organized, and typically either superior to, or completely intertwined with the bureaucratic government organization); (iii) *a terrorist police* (supporting but also supervising the party for its leaders, and characteristically directed not only against demonstrable "enemies" of the regime, but against arbitrarily selected classes of the population); (iv) *a communications monopoly* (a near perfect monopoly of control in the hands of the party and its subservient cadres, of all means of effective mass communication, such as the press, radio, motion pictures); (v) *a weapons monopoly* (a technologically conditioned near-complete monopoly of control (in the same hands) of all means of effective armed combat); (vi) *a centrally directed economy* (through the bureaucratic coordination of its formerly independent corporate entities, typically including most other associations and group activities).[2]

As the authors point out, the last two are also found in (other) constitutional systems: Socialist Britain had a centrally directed economy, and all modern states possess a weapons monopoly. However, they hold the syndrome of all six traits to be typical to totali-

[1] C. J. Freidrich and Z. K. Brezinski, *Totalitarian Dictatorship and Autocracy*, p. 5.
[2] *Ibid.*, pp. 9–10 (quoted in condensed form)

tarian dictatorships. To these points one more may be added here: *collectivism* as the principle of the ideology (theory) as well as of government (practice). The fact that an ideology containing a chiliastic utopian claim requires a holistic view of that society already tends to underemphasize the impact of individual personalities upon the course of social processes, holding these to be dependent on some objective (or mystical) law or principle to which individuals are subordinate. Putting a utopian and holistic scheme into practice requires a political programme (backed by a suitably centralized organization and system of control) which is equally holistic, and powerful enough to eliminate opposition from any individual or factional group within the organization. Neither the ideology, nor the regime of a totalitarian dictatorship is operative or even possible on a principle other than collectivism. Democratic individualism is obviously opposed to holistic planning and action, while aristocratic individualism could produce Autocracies Tyrannies and Oligarchies on the motto of "L'état, c'est moi" applied to the autocrat, tyrant or the ruling minority, but not, however, totalitarian dictatorships.

The main reason for this fact may well lie in the inability of an essentially stratified social system to infuse a spirit of national cohesion and unity of purpose, which is necessary for the effective exercise and maintenance of totalitarian power. Hence we may add the seventh feature to the syndrome of traits characterizing totalitarian dictatorships, the one which is a precondition of its typical ideology and a major factor in the operation of its controls and monopolies: *collectivism, as the ontological principle of social life.*

Although we affirm that totalitarian dictatorship has been and is, the typical form of state of collectivism, we do not exclude the possibility that collectivism may find other operative constitutional forms. Indeed, Israel has proved at least the short-range feasibility of institutionalizing collectivism without a totalitarian dictatorial form, and the growing tendency among many still underdeveloped nations toward socialism without the Marxist-Leninist Party-system testifies to the justification of the prognosis that collectivism on a non-Communist, and non-totalitarian basis might one day be a political fact. Totalitarian dictatorship has evolved in Fascist and Communist countries as the sole means of institutionalizing and maintaining the particular practices prescribed by their ideologies. That a totalitarian dictatorship was found to be necessary for this purpose does not mean that the basic principle of collectivism may only be propagated by such means, but rather that the interaction of ideology and popular political thought made more liberal measures inapplicable. For, in the final count, totalitarianism and collectivism are as incompatible as Democracy and totalitarianism are. The difference on this point is merely that collectivism, by virtue of its fundamental premiss, *permits* totalitarianism as a temporary measure, while Democracy abhors it on all counts and for all occasions. Thus the totalitarian dictatorship of Fascism and Communism could develop as a temporary measure, ostensibly leading to a utopian society where absolutism is either unnecessary or intolerable on principle. In the meanwhile pungent contradictions obtain between the ideology of these systems, and their practice. The essential contradiction of Communism lies in the theoretical affirmation of the determination of individual being by social existence, which, coupled with a hierarchical social practice, implies the unequality of people in Communist society. The logical conclusion derived from the combination of theory and practice is that social existence determines the individual, social existence is hierarchical (the hierarchy ranging from the Party boss to the non-Party member), *ergo* individual being is hierarchical in Communist societies. This conclusion would signify, however, the return to the stratification of Aristocracy, *via* a reversion of the causal determination of individuality and social relations. Thus this conclusion is not admitted, yet the contradiction between theory and practice remains. In view of the fact that such discrepancies are ascribed to the exigencies of specific conditions arising in the present "transistory" phase of Socialist construction, and considering that their resolution may well spell the difference between popular support of, and active opposition to the politics of the Party, the long range stability of the Communist system appears to be dependent to a large extent on the degree to which Communist ideology and social reality can be harmonized, and the utopia translated into reality.

(B) APPLICATIONS – The political thinking of a nation forms a constant dialogue with the political programme of the government and the ontological principle upon which the nation's institutions rest. Institutionalized principles may affect only the people's idea of society, although the idea of general reality entertained by the majority may also be exposed to their influence. It is likely that not more than the popular idea of society is affected (a) when the institutionalized principles and the programme the institutions support and operate merely imply, but do not attempt to explicate the nature of reality beyond the societal, and (b) when the individual makes no specific effort to systematize his *Weltanschauung* through bringing his idea of society in tune with his idea of general reality.

A doctrine of social organization which deals with no more than *social* reality leaves the individual free to think of general reality as he pleases. (A conscious effort to account for society and nature in common terms is seldom undertaken by the average person owing to the great qualitative differences manifested by these areas of experience). On the other hand if the institutionalized, official principle of a society transcends the sphere of societal experience and posits a view of general reality that checks with the propagated idea of society, the influence of the ontological principle will be felt directly on the general ontology of the person: the acceptance of the social doctrine involves then the acceptance of the total ontological doctrine as well. Hence proportionately to the positive influence the nation's institutions exercise upon its people, the ontological *Weltanschauung* typifying the nation will also be affected. Thus a holistic doctrine is likely to affect the *Weltanschauung* of the people, while more delimited principles tend to influence merely the people's idea of social reality.

Political thought, even the conception of general reality, may be induced to follow a prescribed pattern and make use of specific concepts and ideas. While the bases of political thought are the social experience of the individual, that experience may be restructured by an institutionalized principle, and the historical-social conditions of a nation can be altered by a planified system of organization. In addition, the presentation of the ontological principle as an absolutist ideology may intensify and reinforce the spontaneous effect of the changes in everyday experience, by describing each modification as desirable and foreseen. Although liberal societies tend to develop a consciousness of the privacy of being, and planified societies give rise to a sense of the publicity of human existence, both types of thinking remain open to further influence, not excluding the possibility of a transformation if and when the institutionally adopted principle changes. In the long range view it seems unquestionable that popular political thought can be engaged to support a given ontological principle as long as the regime is capable of synchronizing the nation's general type of social experience with the principle upon which the order is built. In the case of liberal societies, not bound to dogmatized foundations, a change in the popular idea of society may provoke corresponding changes in the state apparatus through legislative, parliamentary measures. In totalitarian states the problem of keeping popular political thought loyal to the ideas represented by the leadership is the problem of keeping the advocated principles abreast of social experience. This may be effected by interpreting the principles to fit freshly evolved situations, and by controlling the evolution of events to correspond to the tenets of the advocated doctrine. It is evident, however, that both methods have final limitations.

Balancing the ontological principle embodied by institutions with the dynamic evolution of popular political thought is a particularly problematic task in contemporary societies, where the tempo of evolution has been greatly intensified on all levels. Yet long-range stability for a regime is only possible by achieving a degree of harmony between leadership programmes and public opinion. The rapid evolution of the latter has given rise to radical changes in the form and spirit of constituted states, leading in much of the technologically civilized world from feudal Aristocracy to either Democracy or to Socialism.

The above scheme has been developed to permit the analysis of divergent social and political systems to common, universally human bases. The subsequent analyses will be devoted to the exploration of the conflict of individualism and collectivism, as well as to the definition of the relation of each political principle to political power in specific historical-social settings.

PART II

ANALYSES

I

COMMUNISM: THE INSTITUTIONALIZED THEORY

(i) Structure

The political theory representing the greatest single force in the contemporary world is Marxist-Leninist Collectivism. While Individualism is mostly implicit in the structure of progressive liberal societies, and is given divergent interpretations, Communism represents the institutionalization of a single body of thought. This discussion is devoted to the analysis of Marxism-Leninism in the light of the concepts of individual being and social existence, and the ontology of society that results from their combination. We hope to illuminate thereby the aspect of Communism which represents its long-range force – and perhaps its weakness as well – for whatever other propositions Marxism-Leninism may contain, its concept of man and its idea of society are the immediately effective factors in the political thinking of the masses who are exposed to its tenets. As previously discussed, an interaction obtains in every organized society between the institutionalized ontological principle of state, and the political thinking of the people. The interaction in Communist societies occurs between the ontological principle of Marxism-Leninism and popular political thought. However, owing to the encompassing range of Marxism-Leninism, and its totalitarian application, the interaction may involve not only the political thinking, but also the entire *Weltanschauung* of the people. In fact, under the definition we advance of "ideology" contemporary Marxism-Leninism qualifies for the predicate: it is *systematic, holistic, propagated*, and *institutionalized*. Since this ideology is applied regardless whether its ontological principle is intrinsic to the national idea of society or not, and it is applied as the only valid social, economic, political and philosophical doctrine, Communist societies derive their practice from the dogmatized theory, rather than the theory from the practice. Hence the actual policy of these societies is determined by the ideology, and is only conditioned by local historical-social factors. Nevertheless, the success of Communism – as that of every other political doctrine based on a defined (or definable) ontological idea of society-depends upon the acceptance, tolerance, or at the least on the lack of active opposition, of and by the great masses. As a consequence the ultimate, long-range efficacy of the ideology will be proven or disproven by the effect it has on the local, historical-social conditions which, in the last analysis, determine the political thought of the people. For this reason the critical point of the ideology is its idea of society, the factor which acts directly, as well as through the restructuring of the empirical pattern of social experience, upon the political thinking of the people. Marxism-Leninism proposes a highly explicit idea of society, an idea moreover, which takes an extreme unilateral position with respect to the primacy of society and the individual, and has, as a consequence, an unmistakable, immediately identifiable concept of man. The purpose of our analysis is to show how the Communist idea was born, what the factors were which influenced its formulation, and how the entire structure of the ideology has been constructed to accord with this central political idea. This is an evaluative analysis, an inquiry not only into proposed statements, but also into the meaning of the propositions in the context of the particular setting in which they were formulated, and to which they apply.

Communism advocates a full explanation of reality. Thus we may speak of an essential base and a series of superstructures of the ideology (the latter still leaving "emply domains" of thought [1] but there can be no talk of a limitation in the scope of its relevance.

The Communist ideology is based on the theories of Marx, Engels and Lenin. Soviet philosophers have changed some aspects of these thoughts but have not touched the dogmatized foundation.[2] Since the basic thought is that of Marx, further developed in some respects by Engels and primarily interpreted rather than changed by Lenin, we must have recourse to Marx, in order to analyse the essential structure of Communism (rather than the specific form which its theories are given today).

The life of Marx is adequately treated in several thorough biographical studies and thus we may take here merely those of its aspects which are relevant to the development of his idea of society.

---

[1] As suggested by A. Buckholz (cf. footnote to p. 108).

[2] For the dogmatic and the changeable parts of the integral ideology cf. J. M. Bochenski, "The Three Components of Communist Ideology," *Studies in Soviet Thought*, Vol. II, No. I.

We shall base our inquiry on Marx's activities, as well as on his theories. These two factors cannot be separated, since each conditions the other in every man's political thinking.

Perhaps the first relevant datum on the influences acting upon Marx's thinking in his childhood is his father's hatred of the word "ideology." Hirschel Marx was to have referred with great animation to this "marvellous term ideology." [1] The atmosphere in which Karl Marx grew up was bourgeois, but charged with the existential problems of the day. The effect of these preoccupations in the family can be clearly read from the final examination ("abitur") paper of young Marx: "We cannot always attain the position to which we feel ourselves to be called; the determination of our situation in society is already to some extent under way before we would be capable of deciding it for ourselves." [2] (This is perhaps the first sign of Marx's subsequent theory of historical necessity.) As a student at the University of Berlin, first in the faculty of Law, later in Philosophy, he became a member of the quasi-political "Stralau Graduates Club." No doubt under the influence of his social-political experiences, Marx seceded from the philosophies of Kant and Fichte to that of Hegel. He took position in the camp of the Hegelian left. The Hegelian left, in spite of its philosophical thinking, was interested less in the abstract problems of philosophy in the Aristotelian sense (i.e. in empirical observation and objective explanation), than in the actual problems facing their society. At first this faction remained loyal to the Hegelian cult of the Idea of State, and to its concrete embodiment, the Prussian State. At this point Marx was still positively influenced by the ontological principle of his society; the turn came only later, when he identified himself with the standpoint of a specific class and adopted its judgment. When this turn came the loss of faith in the principle upon which the Prussian State was built was immediately reflected in his philosophical thinking. His doctoral dissertation on *The Distinction between the Democritean and Epicurean Philosophies of Nature* (1841) gives a clear preference for the Epicurean view of the world, despite the greater clarity and precision of Democritus' system. The primary

---

[1] "Den tollen Ausdruck von Ideologie," cf. F. Mehrling, *Karl Marx*, Zürich, 1946, pp. 24. It should be noted that Marx himself used the word in a pejorative sense; it was only in more recent times that Soviet philosophers applied the word to Communist theory. (cf. Tugarinov for example, who writes: "We call ideology not only a system of incorrect ideas, but also a system of correct, scientific ideas as, for instance "Communist ideology'." (*Sootnošenie kategorij istoričeskogo materializma*, 1958, p. 82).
[2] Written on the topic *Betrachtung eines Jünglings vor der Wahl eines Berufs* (1835).

reason for this lies in the Epicurean explanation not only of the material existence of the atom, but also of its form. In addition to the atom's mere givenness, Epicurus leaves the door open to a definition of its essence. To Democritus the material atom was the end, to Epicurus only the means – the end was a view of nature, which the atom theory was to hypostatize. Here Marx's increasing problems in the sphere of social existence found a support. Nature can not only be described and explained, but it can also be *interpreted*. With the help of such heuristic methods human reason can have an effect on the world, but most of all on human destiny, on the world of man and society. Critical theory is to be supplemented by practical activity. The clearest explanation of his preference for the Epicurean type of philosophy was given by Marx later, in his *Theses on Feuerbach*. There we read that "The chief defect of all hitherto existing materialism – that of Feuerbach included – is that the thing (Gegenstand), reality, sensuousness, is conceived only in the form of the *object* (Object) or of *contemplation* (Anschauung), but not as human sensuous activity, practice, not subjectively" (Thesis I). In this proposition Marx offers undisputable evidence of a relational, subjective mode of comprehension, one that permitted him to formulate his interpretation of history, leading ultimately to the Communist utopia where human-sensuous activity triumphs and the relations of all persons are fully coordinate within the social complex.

The precondition for the Marxian *Weltanschauung*, i.e. a subjective evaluation of human activity and human values, was thus already given in the thought of the young Marx.

Marx did not contend himself with theoretical contemplation, but, following his political convictions, entered into the arena of practical politics by contributing articles to Rüge's *Jahrbücher*. He expressed the desire in his articles, to face the problems of the times, rather than to engage in abstract theorizing. Marx became increasingly preoccupied with economic and social questions, and these problems resulted in a shift in his thinking. The evolution of his thought perfectly illustrates our previous contention concerning the influence of historical-social factors on political thought. If we take Marxian thought as primarily action-bound, i.e. by virtue of its ultimate aim practical, political, rather than abstract and intellectual thought, then we will note the influence of historical factors coming into conflict with the influence of social factors in his mind. Historical influence for Marx, was most of all the influence of Hegel. The intellectual milieu of Marx was Hegelian, the atmosphere at Berlin University was clearly dominated by the thought and personality of that philosopher, whom many have criticized, but whom no one could disregard. Young Marx the philosopher, was a Hegelian, belonging to the Hegelian Left in Berlin. Young Marx, the political thinker, was far from being a Hegelian, however. Although the class of Marx was the intelligentsia, as many young intellectuals, Marx preferred to associate his spirit with the oppressed proletariat. Thus the social influences acting on Marx's thought, were those that acted on the proletarians of his times. Since he belonged to an intellectual milieu himself, the concepts and patterns of thought available to Marx were other than those available and current among the proletariat. As the historical influences of Marx's proper class were primarily Hegelian, and the social influences of his adopted class were intensely dissatisfactory, Marx used the concepts of his class to express the judgment of the proletariat: he transformed historical influences into suitable instruments for revolutionary objectives.

Thus the hypothesis proposed above,[1] that as a general rule history conditions the selection of the concepts, and social experience tends to determine the judgment, is clearly confirmed by the Marxian "inversion" of Hegelian philosophy, to serve the cause of the proletariat, rather than that of the Prussian State. The inversion took the form of refuting Hegel's view of the relationship between history and spirit, and instead of subjecting history to the unfolding of the spirit, Marx referred history to the development of material, concrete (rather than ideal) factors. He objects that Hegel treats everywhere the Idea as subject, and thus converts what is actually the subject – man, society – into the predicate. As a result politics becomes a branch of logic, instead of being a practical activity, dealing with concrete, real subjects.

The Prussian State, hypostatized by Hegelian philosophy as the highest expression of ethical life, a superior stage in the unfolding of the Idea, became for Marx a reactionary, fallacious social order: he held it to be an alienation of man's true collective potential, an "abstract collectivity," a thing apart, opposed to the genuine embodiment of human lives, as a governing institution and bureaucracy. Hegelian philosophy was turned "the right side up" according to Marx, and became transformed from a conservative into a revolutionary political doctrine, as a result of Marx's alliegance to the cause of the then revolutionary proletariat. In fact, Marx inverted the historical

[1] cf. p. 35.

thought of his milieu to fit the pattern of social experience he chose to adopt.

By using Hegelian philosophy in an inverted form, he could consider each person a concrete material being, who is nevertheless determined by the collectivity. Such is the concept of "socialized man," the "genuine member of the species."

Since Marx was using a predominantly subjective type of comprehension with respect to societal reality, considering human *being* essentially relationally determined, he needed concepts of being to give substance to his fundamentally existentialist mode of thinking. The egological character of subjective comprehension had to be removed from the sphere of consciousness, and placed on a concrete basis, where it could apply not only to the subject, but also to all humanity, and, given a monistic ontology, to all "being" as well.[1] Marx found what he wanted in Feuerbach's *Essence of Christianity*. Engels described the effect of this work on Marx and his circle in his tract on Feuerbach: "Then came Feuerbach's *Essence of Christianity*. With one blow it pulverized the contradiction, in that without circumlocution it placed materialism on the throne again... We all became Feuerbachians. How enthusiastically Marx greeted the new conception and how much – in spite of all critical reservations – he was influenced by it, one may read in *The Holy Family*." [2]

Marx found that Feuerbach's materialism provides an ideal concept for placing his ego-bound subjective viewpoint on a firm objective footing. Materialistic anthropologism, with its denial of the supernatural, of a Will or Power other than man's, could present the thinker's own experience as the highest criterion of truth and ethics. However, materialistic anthropologism was not enough in itself to *change* the condition of humanity, even if it went a long way toward explaining it. Marx formed a utopian idea of society – expressed in his "alienation" theory – and was therefore not content to explain society; he wanted to change it. To change a society, representing existing material forces, he needed a suitable theory, for he held that material force must be overthrown by material force, and "theory too, becomes a material force, as soon as it takes hold of the masses." In developing a theory capable of becoming a material force in the life of society, the problematic of social existence came ever more to the fore in Marx's thinking, at the expense of empirical observation and objective

---

[1] Marx's problem was, in a sense, to transform an experiential "*Lebenswelt*" into a "natural universe" by deducing objective criteria from subjective comprehension.

[2] F. Engels, *Ludwig Feuerbach*, Marx-Engels, *Selected Works* (*MESW*) II, pp. 332–3.

judgment. The social problematic for Marx was the emancipation of the proletariat, and it was for this purpose that he attempted to develop a theory which he expected, could become a material force aiding social reform. However, mere parliamentary reform was not possible under the conditions obtaining at that time; a revolution appeared to be the *sine qua non* of the proletariat's emancipation. Hence Marx's theory was openly revolutionary in character and stated principles. He envisaged the social revolution wherein the exploited proletariat will abolish private property (not having sizeable properties itself, abolishment of property would thus mean the equalization of the status of the proletariat with that of other classes) and, by making collective property into a basic political principle, create a new type of society. This society would be Communist, and signify the return of man to his essential self in and by a social order which permits individuals to exist as true socialized human beings.

A revolutionary theory requires radical concepts to substantiate its premises. Historical influence, in the form of Hegelian philosophy, supplied such a concept: dialectics. Hegel's dialectics proved to be the ideal concepts not only for explaining, but also for *changing* the existing order. Dialectics could function as a revolutionary thesis when the proletariat is identified with one pole of the dialectical forces motivating human society, and the leading bourgeoisie with the other. One pole, the antithesis, is committed to the task of destroying the other, the thesis, and in the process it is itself transcended. Out of the struggle of thesis and antithesis emerges synthesis, representing a new quality. Society being material (i.e. constituted by the material existence of socialized human beings) the opposites are the propertied, and the exploited, classes. The proletariat will abolish private property, abolishing thereby propertied classes as such, undergoing in the process a qualitative change since it is no longer the exploited class, and usher in the transformation of the social world by keeping all property collective.

In having taken the incentive for materialism from Feuerbach and added the dialectics of Hegel to it, Marx gave evidence of a tendency to incorporate philosophy into his conception of history. Now history in the sense in which Marx understood it, evidently is the history of social existence. This is best illustrated by his theses expounded in the famous introduction to the *Critique of Political Economy*. "In the social production which men carry on they enter into definite relations that are indispensable and independent of their will; these relations of production correspond to a definite stage of development of their material powers of production. The sum total of these relations of production constitutes the economic structure of society – the real foundation on which rise legal and political superstructures and to which correspond definite forms of social consciousness. The mode of production in material life determines (*bedingt*) the general character of the social, political, and spiritual processes of life." [1]

It is obvious that for Marx history concerns the development of the collective processes of life, rather than individuals (as in the more usual conception of history, where motive forces are sought in the analysis of individual personages, their actions, and the ideas which lead them to act). For Marx the individual taken in abstraction from his relations to society (in his economic determinism, to the material forces operating in society) is incomplete, and in the final analysis impossible – man is a socialized being, and not an individual one.

The theory of the individual developed by Marx is a complex one, having two opposing poles of reference. On the one side Marx is an ontological (though never a political) individualist: he gives priority to the particular over the universal, to the concrete over the abstract, to the real over the ideal. Although Marx himself uses the term "materialism" to define his ontological standpoint, it is possible to construe it as a form of individualism. His ontological standpoint is particularly clearly expounded in his "Kritik des Hegelsche Staatsrechts (1843).[2] He opposes Hegel, whom he criticizes for taking the predicate as the subject, and introducing thereby "mysticism" into the theory of State. For Marx the subject is prior and its qualities are merely the predicates, as opposed to Hegel, for whom the predicate (the idea) is embodied as the real subject. Considered from the viewpoint adopted by Marx in this work, one could expect him to develop a social theory allied to the principle of individualism. This was not the case, however. Marx's ontological individualism was first of all a reaction against Hegelian idealism, which made it impossible to place a subjective evaluation of existential experience on an objective, sociological footing. The priority of the universal had to be cut down to size, and subordinated to the particular, since it is the particular person who judges reality according to his needs and practical experiences. Hence only two years later, in 1845, Marx allied his theoretical individualism with an equally theoretical collectivism, in stating

---

[1] Karl Marx, *Zur Kritik der politischen Ökonomie*, Stuttgart, 1857.

[2] *Aus der Kritik der Hegelschen Rechtsphilosophie*, Marx-Engels, *Historisch-kritische Gesamtausgabe (MEGA)*, see particularly paragraph 279.

that "the human essence is no abstraction inherent in each single individual. In its reality it is the ensemble of social relations." "The standpoint of the old materialism is *"civil"* society; the standpoint of the new is *human* society, or socialized humanity." [1] Hence Marx's individual is a complex entity: it is neither an abstract being possessing its own essence, nor a relational being deriving completely from a collectivity; it is both. The concrete reality (materiality) of the person is proper to himself, and is prior to his external coordinations. The qualities of the person, however (his humanity, essence) is secondary to the collectivity, being determined by the (social) relations of the individual. These two superimposed layers correspond to Aristotelian, and to Hegelian philosophy, the Marxian theory signifying an attempt at their synthesis. Our contention is that, by affirming the concrete reality of the person, and then subordinating his qualities to society, Marx was motivated by the necessity of finding the apposite theoretical framework for the interpretation of the sphere of objective being in the subjective light of an experience of social existence. The combination of realistic individualism with essentialist collectivism provided the basis for the cosmological interpretation of human, as well as of general reality. The history of humanity represents for Marx neither the evolution of individuals only (in the Aristotelian sense) nor purely the evolution of the social collectivity (in the Hegelian sense). History embraces the development of socialized humanity, the development of a species of material entity with a collective essence. Since this species is not isolated from the rest of reality, but lives in its framework, nature as the general sphere of concrete real entities, must obey the same laws and manifest the same essential characteristics as socialized humanity. The standpoint of Marx is a clearly defined philosophical monism. It led him to conclude that man is a part of nature, and that nature as a whole is material and subject to the laws of dialectics in all its dynamic manifestations. There is no opposition between man and nature, for notwithstanding his highly evolved mental powers, man's primary activity is material, not spiritual: he produces real objects, and in so doing puts his energies – in fact, himself – into them. Thus a mutual dependence between man and nature obtains, wherein man has the upper hand. Marx affirms that the adjustment of nature to human need furnishes the content of history. Man struggles to adapt nature to his requirements, and in the process comes to adapt himself to nature – this two-fold adaptation

---

[1] *Theses on Feuerbach* VI, X.

is the nucleus of the concept of "practice" for Marx. It is highly significant that the adaptive processes are based on the cognition of objects in the context of utility for a practical purpose, rather than on the comprehension of objects and processes as they are presented to the senses. Hence the concept of practice, and with it the content of history, is represented by a subjective mode of comprehending the environment.

Subjective evaluation and objective being are essentially incompatible: subjective comprehension could only be the foundation of objective knowledge if perceptive and cognitive processes could be shown to reflect, represent, or in some way equal things and events outside consciousness. Marx developed the dialectical theory of knowledge in answer to this problem. Dialectical materialist epistemology, further evolved by Lenin, functions to equate knowledge attained through practice (i.e. subjectively) with objective reality. The theory can be summarized in capsule form, by the basic propositions that: (i) matter is primary, and thought (spirit) secondary, derived from matter; (ii) reality is material and matter dialectic, hence matter evolves dialectically from lower to higher forms; as a result reality is intelligible; (iii) matter has the property of reflection, i.e. of entering into dynamic interrelations; the thought of man is the reflection of objective reality by a higher evolved material entity, derived from sense-knowledge by virtue of its highly sensitive organ of thought (the brain); consequently thought is dialectical, it being the subjective reflection of an objective dialectical process. It follows then that (iv) practice attained in the course of history is true knowledge, and the only criterion of any theory's validity.[1]

By affirming the presence of dialectics in the world of the mind, and attributing it to a reflection of real, objective dialectical processes, the bridge between practice as the basis of knowledge, and matter as the basis of being has been erected. The harmonious sweep of the theory is marred only by the consideration that once the Hegelian system is broken by materialist realism, the assertion of dialectical thought processes is as lacking in conviction as the assumption of objective dialectical processes is. A further unpleasing implication is the evident reduction of psychic phenomena to physical ones, and the equation of an ontological, with a psycho-physical problem. These are correlates of the complexity of the being of the Marxian individual,

---

[1] For recent Soviet work on the dialectical materialist theory of knowledge see T. J. Blakeley, *Soviet Theory of Knowledge*, Dordrecht (in prep.).

an individual whose concrete reality is prior, but whose essence is secondary, to the collectivity. Consciousness, coming under the heading of essence, thus "can never be anything else than conscious existence... Life is not determined by consciousness, but consciousness by life." [1] "It is not the consciousness of men that determines their existence, but, on the contrary, their social existence determines (*bestimmt*) their consciousness." [2]

The postulate, advanced earlier,[3] concerning the determination of the view of consciousness by the basic approach to the problem of reality is confirmed by Marx: the basic premiss of "practice" as the touchstone of knowledge led him to the proposition that the essential content of consciousness is social. The inference, in itself logical and necessary, was justified by invoking the principle of Hegelian dialectics.

But, in a sense the use of dialectics defeated the Marxian revolt against Hegel. Marx started his philosophical career under the influence of Hegel, revolted against him (on primarily sociopolitical grounds) and was forced back to the Hegelian position by the use of the dialectical principle. Although Marx was concerned with the fate of the individual, his conception of society as determinant of personality found dialectics well suited to express his subjective viewpoint, and led eventually to the subordination of the individual to the collectivity, notwithstanding the original, mainly moral, motivation.[4]

Dialectics as the central principle of ontology and epistemology sees the motive force of all being and all knowledge in contradictions: contradiction is the essence of all reality, and the principle of cosmic evolution. Now contradiction is essentially a relational concept, for contradiction obtains when contradictory principles are brought into effective interrelational nexus. In that sense all relations are external to the moments of contradiction, but since contradiction is inherent in each entity, these dialectical external relations are also internal with respect to the essence of the being-becoming of all things. The essence of all being is thus given by the relations obtaining between the relations of contradictory poles; the individual as abstract being is null, unexistent and unimaginable. *Das Wahre ist das Ganze* said Hegel, summing up his idea of a world-embracing universal interconnection and interdetermination of all things.

---

[1] *MEGA*, pt. I. 5. pp. 15 f.
[2] *Zur Kritik der Politischen Ökonomie* (Introduction).
[3] cf. p. 18.
[4] Marx's original concern over the individual is evidenced also by his admiration of Epicurus in his youth.

Applied to the level of humanity the Hegelian dialectical synthesis involves the objective spirit (the spirit of the collectivity) finding expression in law, morality and ultimately in ethical life, and the subjective spirit (the spirit of the individual, the person) as the vehicle for the objective spirit of the group. This permits Hegel to analyse human consciousness as psychologically and anthropologically collective-determined: the synthesis of the objective and subjective spirit gives rise to the Absolute Spirit, existing not merely "in-itself" (as the objective spirit) but also "for-itself." The view of society resulting from the acceptance of dialectics as the principle of being and evolution terminates in the affirmation of the primacy of the collectivity as the relevant "whole" of human life. The individual represents merely dialectical moments in the existence of the collective whole, hence the individual has no autonomy, no individuality, other than the one lent to him by his cosmic locus. An individual can never be entirely that which he is in abstraction, for his relations determine his essence, his thinking, and ultimately, his being.

The real existent is the relational network wherein particulars find themselves and of which they are parts, the subject is always a determined moment of the substance of the relational complex. Thus Hegel's conception of the relation of the individual to the collectivity signifies total (metaphysical) collectivism. In accepting dialectics as the principle of objective being and development and substituting materialism in place of Hegel's idealism, Marx affirmed the primacy of matter over spirit. Having posited the secondary nature of the world of thought, he was obliged to subordinate it to the laws which prevail in the "material" world: dialectics is applicable then to the mind as it is to the body. If the body is subject to dialectical interrelations with the universe as a whole, the mind is determined by the reflection of this interdeterminational process. Hence the mind is in fact nothing other than the conscious awareness (to a greater or lesser degree) of the dialectical processes which determine the being of the individual. If dialectical laws regulate the individual's being, then these laws are the laws of the organic processes taking place within the individual on the one hand (of these, however, the mind has no direct experiential knowledge) and the organic processes occurring externally to the individual but within the collectivity on the other – these form the individual's daily experience, and are thus determinant of his consciousness. As the humanity (though not the material reality) of the individual is one moment in the complex dialectical relations obtaining in the collectivity, his mind reflects one specific standpoint: it is the conceptualization of one pole in the social dialectic. Each dialectical relationship involves two moments (the thesis and the antithesis) and in society these are represented by two general classes of relational social standpoints: the exploited and the exploiting class. The consciousness of the individual reflects the consciousness of his class; consciousness is not an individual, but a social attribute, it is *classconsciousness*.

Although Marx revolted against the Hegelian subordination of individual values to the social collectivity (incorporated for Hegel by the Prussian State, the highest realization of ethical life), in adopting Hegelian dialectics he could not do otherwise than posit the essentiality of relations, and thus return to the point from which he attempted to liberate philosophy (and politics): the worship of collective life.

The revolt against Hegel utilized half-measures: it attempted to discard what was bad and make use of what was valuable. In so doing Marx ignored the thoroughness with which the Hegelian philosophical system is grounded in the method of its exposition; the adoption of one leads necessarily to the re-adoption of the other. Marx attempted to reform Hegel's absolute, metaphysical collectivism by affirming the priority of the individual, but was forced to relinquish his individualism owing to the adoption of the dialectical principle. Thus the Marxian sociological and economic doctrine became fully collectivist, leaving ontological individualism to the natural sciences.

Marx was intensely committed in the social and political issues of his day and this fact sheds light on much of his reasoning. Although it is evident from Marx's works that the orientation of his *Weltanschauung* was already fixed for life in his middle twenties (certainly at the time of his collaboration with Arnold Rüge on the "Rheinischen Zeitung" in Cologne) and his later years served to refine and evolve, but not to change the mode of comprehension on which he based his theories, it is well to recall the interconnection between his activity and thought, by taking account of the milieu in which he created his major works. The *"Deutsch-Französischen Jahrbücher"* are the product of his collaboration with Rüge, in the intensely political atmosphere of the Rheinischen Zeitung, and the Vorwärts, in Paris. Marx's intellectual contacts at this time included H. Heine, Proudon, and for the first time, Engels. He studied French Socialism, Communism, and economic-philosophical problems, until his eviction from France (1845). *"Die Heilige Familie"* and *"Die Deutsche Ideologie"* were created in

Brussels, in collaboration with Engels. During this time (1847) he enlisted in the Communist League, and travelled to London to their conference. A direct resultant of the trip was the *"Communist Manifesto,"* also with Engels" collaboration (1848). Eviction from Brussels followed. Marx assumed the editorship of the "Neuen Rheinischen Zeitung" in Cologne, met with Lassalle and Freiligrath. He went to Vienna to speak at the meeting of the *Wiener Arbeiterverein.* 1849 saw Marx evicted from Cologne and the Neuen Rheinischen Zeitung prohibited. Marx then represented German Democracy in Paris, until he was evicted from there too, and went in exile to London. In London he edited the "Neuen Rheinischen Revue," gave lectures, became correspondent of the "New York Tribune." *"Der 18. Brumaire des Napoleon Bonaparte"* is the product of these times. The dissolution of the Communist League was followed by his collaboration on the "New American Cyclopaedia," correspondence with Lassalle, and in 1859 publication of his famous *"Zur Kritik der Politischen Ökonomie."* Thereafter came the foundation of the International Workers' Association with a meeting in St. Martin's Hall in London (inaugural address), the break with the Allgemeinen Deutschen Arbeiterverein after a short collaboration on Schweitzer's "Sozialdemokraten," conference of the International in London (1865). The First Congress of the International was held in Geneva in 1866, and the year thereafter appeared the first volume of *"Das Kapital."* The same year the Second Congress took place in Lausanne, while the Third followed a year later. 1869 is the date of the *"Konfidentielle Mitteilung"* against Bakunin, as well as of the Fourth Congress in Brussels. Aside from speeches at various meetings and conferences this period gave birth to no major work. Marx was engaged in writing the following volumes of *"Das Kapital"* composed a polemic against Bakunin *"L'alliance de la démocratie socialiste et l'Association internationale des travailleurs"* and was taken seriously ill. The Gotha Programme of the German Workers' Party in 1875 served for the composition of Marx's well known *"Programmkritik."* With that Marx's creative period came to a close. While in 1877 he collaborated with Engels on the latter's *Anti-Dühring*, the work was done by Engels, with Marx functioning mostly in an advisory capacity. Marx died in 1883, without having added to his theories in his last years. The second and third volumes of *"Das Kapital"* appeared in 1885 and 1894, posthumously.

In looking over his creative production Marx's life may be classified roughly into four periods.[1] The first, from his birth in 1818 until he

---

[1] Following a suggestion of J. M. Bochenski.

entered the University of Berlin in 1836, includes his childhood and early intellectual formation. Although he was too young yet to compose books and articles, several indications (among them the *Abitur* paper) exist which testify to his intellectual development. The second period was fertile in ideas: it stretches from the beginning of the Berlin time until his marriage with Jenny v. Westphalen in 1843. Into this period falls Marx's greatest interest for the problems of philosophy, as well as the sharpening of his interest in sociopolitical questions. The third period could be seen to commence with the move to Paris in 1843 and to last until the 1849 eviction from France. These years bear witness to Marx's increasing involvement with sociological and sociopolitical questions. The fourth and final creative period starts with the emigration to London (1849) and ends with the "Gotha Kritik" in 1875. In these years Marx gave himself over to the almost exclusive consideration of political economy, and of the organizational questions connected with the proletarian emancipation movement. The remaining years were spent without marked creative activity, editing past thoughts and further organizing the movements initiated earlier.

This "phase" interpretation of the life of Marx takes on particular significance when we consider that he progressed from philosophy, to sociology and economy, while never abandoning his political interests and activities. As we are dealing with one person, it is reasonable to assume that some kind of intellectual unity, a continuous thread connecting Marx's activities must be given, notwithstanding the different fields wherein they were performed. This thread is evidently *politics*. The political interests of Marx were clearly manifest in his first mature period: his joining the "Stralau Graduates Club" in Berlin (a quasi political organization) and his work on the Rheinischen Zeitung in Köln give undisputable evidence of this. While politics stayed with him until the end of his days, philosophy (while not fully abandoned) gave way to sociology, and finally to political economy in his thoughts. Now it is fairly obvious that his work in sociology and economics was dictated by pragmatic goals: Marx wanted to *do* something, to "change the world." The motive force of these periods is manifestly political. Might it not be that the prime motive force of his philosophical period was also the formulation and crystallization of a political objective? No doubt political objectives were already present in his thinking in Berlin. The question posed here is whether those political objectives were primary, and thus determinant of his philosophical activity, in the same sense as they were determinant later of his interest in sociology and economy? If we admit that behind the great creative powers of Marx the continuous dynamic motivation was politics, more precisely the political goal of bringing about the emancipation of the 19th century German and West European proletariat from its desperate situation, then Marx's life acquires a harmonious unity, notwithstanding his wide-ranging interests. Still more importantly the conclusion emerges that his life (as most other lives spent in creative thinking and activity) represented a continuous and logical process, one, in his case, wherein the constant objective, acting as the main spring of all intellectual and practical activity – the cause of the proletariat – became crystallized through a series of experiments with philosophy, sociology, and finally economy. In that event, Marx's interest in philosophy can be ascribed primarily to the Hegelian atmosphere of the University of Berlin, an atmosphere which linked philosophy with politics owing to Hegel's endorsement of the Prussian State. Given these circumstances a young man of Marx's intellectual abilities and political interests would inevitably be drawn into the sphere of philosophy *as the highest court of politics*. The primary motivation would thus be politics, with philosophy considered as the highest instance for settling political problems, and the concepts and methods of philosophy regarded as the best and clearest tools for conclusive political debates. Had Marx stayed with philosophy throughout his life, his thought could be considered essentially philosophical, even if conditioned and motivated by external factors. However, the interests of Marx turned progressively away from philosophy. He continued using philosophical concepts to substantiate his arguments (for his conceptual equipment was philosophical), but in later years neither the end nor the means was philosophy itself.

If we consider Marx's life as an intellectual *progression* (rather than a regression), then the conclusion emerges that, as his ideas crystallized, philosophy as a means to express his basic objectives was superseded by sociology and economy. In *"Das Kapital,"* for example, we find a mature thinker, whose interests are in economy (in *political* economy, specifically) with hardly a trace of what one might take for pure philosophical speculation or analysis. When the continuous thread in the life of Marx is taken to be his political interest, then philosophy, sociology and economy appear as the intellectual means for clarifying his views and giving them logical, structural form.

Considered as a progression, economy appears as the ultimate apex of Marxian thought, with philosophy taking third place as the representative of a youthful period. A distinction between various periods and fields in Marx's thought can serve to illuminate a general *tendency* (consisting of finely shaded transitions) characterizing the life and thought of a man whose creative production is a major force of our times. The above schema has been pruposely drawn to extremes, in order to afford an insight into delicate processes, having nevertheless distinct characteristics. The question is one of *primacy*, and may be formulated as hinging on the problem of primacy between politics, philosophy, sociology and economics in Marx's intellectual world.[1]

The primacy in Marx's mind of immediate and specific (as distinct from general and intellectual) problems, decides the character of his creative production. And,as we shall show, the primacy of philosophy, sociology, economy, and politics, decides the *validity* of Marxian thought as well.

After this brief excursion into the life and thought of Marx, we shall return to the consideration of the integral structure of the Communist ideology. Marx is rightly considered the founder of the philosophical edifice: the conceptual structure derives almost entirely from his thoughts. Nevertheless, owing to his increasing interest in social and economic questions, the analysis of the implications of his thought to spheres of reality exceeding the societal has been left to others. Engels, his closest friend and collaborator, is responsible for working out the dialectical materialist interpretation of nature. If the integral structure of Communist philosophy is divisible into two parts, dialectical materialism and historical materialism, then Marx's contribution is to Histomat, while Engels' major contribution is to Diamat. (It is Engels' theory of dialectics as a universal ontological law that is promulgated by Soviet philosophers today.) We have attempted to show that Marx was guided in his interpretation of history by political goals, i.e. by his own experiences of social existence and by the idea of society he formulated. Historical, social and political influences were not only evident, but prominent in his thinking. Although Marx developed a social theory, he adopted monism in philosophy, and thus his interpretation of man and society required to be supplemented by a corresponding interpretation of general reality. This was the task Engels set himself. In the joint works of Marx and Engels – *"The*

---

[1] The hypothesis according to which Marx's political interests were motivated by feelings of moral obligation, is not excluded from the argument.

Holy Family" and *"The German Ideology"* they progressed together from the influence of Hegel to the concepts of dialectical materialism. The works dealing with history have preceded the ones dealing with nature, however. This temporal priority is significant when we pose the question of the priority of the subject-matter in their thinking. Engels had the cooperation of Marx in his polemic against Dühring, but his treatise on the *"Dialectics of Nature"* was left unfinished (as the Preface to the Russian edition of 1948 states). Engels was engaged in writing this work from 1873 to 1883, then, however, the death of Marx compelled him to postpone it for more pressing obligations. It was never completed. The chronology of events shows that dialectics was applied by Engels to the investigation of nature after Marx had interpreted history with its help. The respective part the collaborators had in working out the interpretation of nature can be seen from Engels' statement in his *"Ludwig Feuerbach":* "I cannot deny that both before and during my forty years of collaboration with Marx I had a certain independent share in laying the foundations of the theory and more particularly in its elaboration. But the greater part of its leading principles... belong to Marx. What I have contributed – at any rate with the exception of my work in a few special fields – Marx could very well have done without me. What Marx accomplished I would not have achieved." [1]

In applying dialectics to history, Engels kept closely in step with Marx. The application of dialectics to the "few special fields" he mentions above, is very much his own work, however. As Engels explains: "Marx and I were pretty well the only people to rescue conscious dialectics from German idealist philosophy and apply it in the materialist conception of nature and history. But a knowledge of mathematics and natural science is essential to a conception of nature which is dialectical and at the same time materialistic. Marx was well versed in mathematics, but we could only partially, intermittently and sporadically keep up with the natural sciences." [2] Engels applied himself in his later years to overcome this deficiency. He started his investigations with the basic idea that "dialectics is nothing more than the science of the general laws of motion and development in nature, human society and thought." [3]

Engels had in mind to: "convince myself in detail – of what in

[1] F. Engels *Ludwig Feuerbach, MESW,* II, p. 349.
[2] F. Engels, *Anti-Dühring,* p. 15.
[3] Ibid., p. 158.

general I was not in doubt – that amid the welter of innumerable laws taking place in nature, the same dialectical laws of motion are in operation as those which in history govern the apparent fortuitiousness of events." He added that in this "there could be no question of building the laws of dialectics into nature, but of discovering them in it, and evolving them from it." [1]

Engels' attempt can be criticized as being an essay at the explanation of phenomena in terms of concepts which are their hypostatization. The fact that dialectics was applied to nature following its application to thought and history, together with the consideration that the thinking of the investigator was fully biased by that time gives rise to the suspicion that Engels' view of nature was the product of his view of history. Now the Marx-Engels view of history was bound up with their theory of consciousness, and they based these on this experience of social existence. Consequently in the final analysis their view of nature was subjected to existential influences and developed through the use of subjective norms. The same applies to the social and economic doctrines. We must consider that the Marxist interpretation of history and the Marxist economic theory were both based on the premiss of the relational determination of individual consciousness and will. Without the assumption of this definite, predominantly one-way causality between the collectivity and the humanity of the individual, neither the sociological nor the economic doctrine could have been developed in their actual form, and the very essence of Communism – its collectivism – would have been lacking. Thus notwithstanding the manifold facets of Communist thought (many of which have been left out of explicit consideration in this analysis), the ontological principle of Communist society is the determinant feature of the ideology, when it is taken as an active and powerful social agent of our times. It is this aspect that we have attempted to analyze in terms of the previously evolved schematization of the structure of political thought. In summary, the conclusion of the analysis holds Communism's category of *matter* to represent concepts of *objective* being (the ontology of being) while *practice* (as the ground for knowledge and the content of history) as the *subjective* concept that permits the evolution of an ontology of existence.

Dialectics as an epistemological principle, functions primarily to bolster dialectic as the objective principle of material reality. As the ontological principle, dialectics is a *heuristic*, theoretical concept in

[1] Ibid., p. 15.

Marxist philosophy, for the interpretation of being in terms of existence (material being in terms of practice). No doubt the choice of the dialectical principle for this function has been greatly influenced by its ethical connotation, making it capable of validifying a political action programme when removed from the sphere of ideas and applied to that of concrete social existence.[1]

(ii) Validity

Marx lived in a society wherein historical-social conditions produced a spontaneous tendency toward radical social reforms. The relevant features of the conditions were the extreme stratification of the social system, together with a general refusal to admit essentially differing levels of being among the members of different classes. As a result, underprivileged classes saw no justification for their position, and demanded full emancipation. Since the social structure was backed by tradition and supported by a great military and state organization‘ and emancipation meant a social reform contrary to the traditional, accepted order, the movement of the most underprivileged class – the proletariat – was possible only by radical means: social revolution. Revolution meant not only reforming, but completely replacing the existing political system. Now the institutionalized ontological principle of the existing system was aristocratic-individualism. Social reform could have been achieved by either democratic-individualism, or collectivism (socialism). The former means leaving the individualist principle, removing the conception of essential differences from among the private, discrete being of individuals, and reorganizing the social structure on the principle of accidental, secondary differences, tolerating a stratification corresponding to the various capacities and training of individuals for specific public functions, while giving them equal rights as private citizens. Collectivism, on the other hand, means keeping the direct, essential causal nexus between individual being and social existence, but giving priority to existence and hence discarding the individualist ontological principle and replacing it by the collectivist one. Equal rights in collectivism mean equal social relations, and equal valuation of all public functions. Thereby an excessively stratified social system can be radically equalized.

---

[1] Hegelian dialectics removes contradiction from the *Seiende* and the *Seinsollende*, thus validifying the predication of "ought" from "is" through the application of its method. cf. Max Theimer, *Der Marxismus*, ch. II.

Marx was a man of these times. He was fully involved in the socio-political problematic of the day – by nature, upbringing, and intellectual environment he was drawn into an atmosphere which was thoroughly partisan, pledging uncompromisingly allegiance to the cause of the proletariat. Marx well realized that radical measures were likely to be the most efficacious for this cause – the more radical the greater the chance of success. It was clear to him that proceeding by gradual reforms meant revising rather than destroying the actual regime, and revision appeared to be a difficult, perhaps even a hopeless task. Marx chose the radical solution: left-wing socialism. There can be little doubt that he really believed socialism to be the sole means out of the increasingly oppressive problems of the times. He devoted all his activity to furthering the cause of socialism – he was surrounded with people who either believed in his movement, or opposed it. In the effort to strengthen support for the movement and to disarm opposition he made increasing use of arguments, and his arguments could not be based on empirical observation but had to be theoretical: Marx did not want to *explain* the situation, he wanted to *change* it. He formed an idea of society which differed by far from the experience of actual conditions, and he needed an action programme to reduce this differential. To win support the action programme had to be backed by the largest and firmest possible theoretical structure. In wanting to change actual conditions, Marx also wanted to change the ideas his contemporaries entertained of reality; he wanted to change the world by seeing it in a light which showed it essentially good for man and society, and showed contemporary man and contemporary society as temporarily bad, erred from the right path (alienated man and society). The emancipation of the oppressed classes was the road to achieve the good, the natural state of humanity. This meant changing alienated men into socialized men and the present Prussian state into Communist society.

The structure of Marxian thought was based on the primacy of subjective concepts which, borrowing the method from Hegel's metaphysical collectivism, gave rise to the concept of socialized man, an entity whose relational existence determines his individual being. This concept provided the foundation for the idea of Communist society, where all have equal relations to the social whole, all persons function both as public figures and as specialized workers (the State dies away), the private sphere of life is thrown open to the collectivity, and the essential nature of man is fulfilled: Communist society is the natural state of existence of socialized humanity. In order to achieve this ultimate state the present had to be evaluated in terms of an interpretation of the past which shows Communist society to be the natural, inevitable resultant of the general course of social evolution. Such an interpretation of history had to rest on more than the mere description of events: it had to evaluate events in the light of specific criteria. Thus the need for a conceptual framework presented itself. Marx's solution was dialectical evolutionism applied to the central category of matter. These concepts were developed in answer to concrete needs; they functioned to fill the gap between Marx's Communist utopia and his actual social experience. The need was not merely that of an isolated individual, however, but it was shared by an entire class of people in that society. The particular conceptual framework giving rational support to the expression of that need was Marx's work, but insofar as this framework permitted the substantiation of a widely felt need, it was symptomatic of the times. Notwithstanding its theoretical nature it was more than an intellectual abstraction, for it was designed to authenticate and support a practical political action programme, and was thus meant to function as an active social agent. The concepts used to authenticate this political programme were adopted to help eliminate the outmoded and on the whole reactionary forces operating at the time, and determining the course of social events.

If we admit that the Prussian state was superseded by new realities arising from dynamically evolving social conditions, we can predicate the reactionary aspects of the Prussian state false, and whatever serves to eliminate these aspects true. Insofar as Marxian philosophy functioned to authenticate a political programme, and insofar as that political programme served to eliminate the false elements of the actual social system, Marxian philosophy functioned as truth with respect to the defects of the system. Its truth-value was strictly conditional, however, being dependent upon the specific configuration of socio-economic and political conditions typified by the Prussian state.

This does not exclude the truth-value of Marxism Leninism with respect to other historical-social situations, however. While historical-social conditions never repeat exactly in different times and at different places, sufficient similarities may occur to validate the Marxist authentication of a specific political programme in more than one locus. Since minor differences between any two sets of conditions are bound to obtain, the theory has to be "creatively extended" to suit the given terrain. Such extension has occurred with respect to Russia in 1917. There, just as in Germany half a century earlier, an excessive stratification of the social system was coupled with the refusal to see basic differences in the being of the aristocracy and the lower classes, with the result that the latter demanded the egalization of their status, corresponding to their ontological idea of society. Marxist thought was eminently capable of providing full scale authentication to this movement; it could lend it a conception of general reality exactly suited to the viewpoint of the emancipating masses. Lenin, just as Marx earlier, was an intellectual, immersed in the socio-political problematic of his society. He found that Marxian thought applied to Russia, and proceeded to custom tailor it to the peculiarities of the social structure created by the Tsarist regime. Among the many, but nonessential alterations he made, we may note that he revised the concept of the proletariat as the sole motive force of history, proposing its alliance with the peasantry (this was necessary in view of the fact that in agrarian Russia the majority of the emancipating masses belonged to the peasantry); he deepened the concept of matter to prevent new discoveries in the field of natural science from contradicting the assertion of the world's materiality; he made absolute truth (restricted by Marx to practice) attainable theoretically; and he further developed the theory of knowledge by positing that the mind copies, photographs and reflects objective reality. He placed added emphasis on the unity of theory and practice, demanded partisanship in philosophy, and developed the concept of the dictatorship of the proletariat as the theoretical justification of totalitarian government. Despite these alterations the ontological structure of Marxian thought remained unchanged: the concept of man, the idea of societal and general reality, and the political action programme leading to its realization have been preserved. The alterations of Lenin, Stalin, and now of the contemporary theoreticians of the Soviet Union, serve to extend the original theory, and make it applicable to a wider range of conditions. The Soviet ideology is constantly extended by finding new interpretations of the original thesis, validifying the Communist political programme in a more extended range of circumstances. However, when we take the political thought of the majority as the criterion for the validity of political programmes, then each political theory functions as truth only as long as the programme derived from its premisses serves to reduce the differential between the

II

AN ASSESSMENT OF
THE EVOLUTION OF POPULAR POLITICAL
THOUGHT UNDER COMMUNISM

The purpose of this analysis is to assess the effects an exposure to Soviet ideology has on the political thinking of a people. Our main objective is to account for the decisive trends in Communist countries as logical resultants of the interaction of the Communist ideology and local historical-social conditions in the idea the broadest masses form of society.

The idea of society is universally human and open to influence. The Communist ideology represents one such idea (an extreme form of it), but it is propagated as the absolute and uncontestable truth, not tolerating contradictions or even qualifications. Hence we have two social ontologies interacting in Soviet-dominated societies: the Communist idea of society and the social ideas of the masses. These ontologies are brought into effective and constant contact by the ideological work of the Party; consequently the representative political thought of all Communistic countries must be the resultant of an osmosis of the two elements. As the ideology's effect is conditioned by the historical-social pattern of experience in the minds of the people and as this pattern is transformed through the Communist political programme, an intricate interplay results, which it is well worth examining. We shall distinguish three phases: the first being characterized by the infiltration of the Communist idea of society in the social consciousness, the second by the strife between the nationalist and internationalist ways of realizing this idea in practice, and the third by the potential erosion of the ontological principle of Communist society.

The First Phase

Every institutionalized political principle tends to propagate and conserve the ontological premiss upon which it is built. Aristocratic-individualism could successfully propagate an idea of society based on a hierarchy of individual being, and giving rise to a social hierarchy of existence, until the lower and middle strata began thinking of themselves as the equals of their social superiors and thus felt slighted by the social order. When these feelings developed sufficient momentum, social reforms took place, either by radical revolutionary means, or by more gradual parliamentary measures. Aristocratic-individualism is so far the only one of the three principal varieties of the ontological principles we have distinguished, that appears to be definitely superseded in all the socio-economically advanced areas of the globe. The two other ontological principles of social organization – collectivism and democratic-individualism – are its successors, and are hence newcomers on the scene. This discussion is devoted to the reconstruction of the processes permitting the development of collectivism in a given nation when its ontological principle is institutionalized, and propagated under full ideological pressure.[1]

Since there are no public opinion surveys or other wide-scale efforts made in the countries of the Soviet bloc to ascertain just how far the Communist idea has penetrated into the genuine political thinking of the people, precise documentation of the first phase in the evolution of popular political thought under Communism is lacking. However, the lack of evidence contradicting the assumption of the effective infiltration of the Communist idea is itself a significant proof in favour of it. There has been no spontaneous uprising in any Communist dominated country that could be ascribed to a full counterrevolutionary movement. Uprisings and revolts have been many, but none voiced a desire to "return" to the "bourgeois" way of life. These conflicts have been much more due to conflicting views as to the best road to take to realize the Communist idea of society. It would be too much to say that this idea is ever precisely the one dreamt of by Marx and Engels in the Communist Manifesto and now heralded by the promises of the Third Programme of the CPSU. But there is no doubt that the idea is always a collectivist one, and that it resulted from exposure to the Marx-Engels-Lenin conception of Communist society.[2]

Another strand of evidence testifying to the effectiveness of the infiltration of this idea into social consciousness in Communist countries reaches us through interviews with persons who have lived under

[1] The correspondence of Communist ideas and political institutions is affirmed by the Soviet ideologues, themselves (cf. the textbooks *Osnovy Marksizma-Leninizma*, and *Istorichesky Materializm*, Moscow).

[2] The term "Communist idea of society" is used henceforth to indicate the general collectivist idea engendered in the masses by Marxism-Leninism.

Communism for a number of years. These persons give clear evidence of having a "utopian" mentality, i.e. thinking in terms of a future society, toward which the present is merely a phase of transition. Furthermore this future society is always envisaged as a collectivist one, where equality means not merely equal individual rights and equal chances for advancement, but also a unilateral social structure wherein all people are considered equal by virtue of their public function. The source of inegality in the West is seen by these people as the concentration of private property in certain classes, making the members of the propertied classes something fundamentally different from the unpropertied workers. The clash of their interests is reflected in the conflict of their consciousness, and in the final analysis in the opposition of their basic natures (i.e., their individual beings). Out of this conflict they believe, comes social progress, and eventually a brighter future.

The western mentality differs from this type of thinking in that it does not place the social ideal in the future and think of the present as merely a difficult period of transition, but considers that whatever form of society is realized today is already valid as an expression of man's social strivings and does not need to be taken merely as a transitory phase. In other words, social evolution is conceived here as a continuous and more or less straightforward process (rather than a dialectical one), full value is attributed to the present, while the future is held to be incapable of being fully ascertained, although it is assumed that it lies in the direction that has been taken by mankind in its past history. Most of all, the general (though often tacit) conviction of the western mind is the belief in the coincidence of individual and collective good, with the good of the *individual* as criterion. It is assumed that whatever I, as a person pursuing my own goals, looking for my own happiness, do (insofar as I do not break any laws) coincides with the goals and ultimate interests of my society. I work for society by working for myself, and if I arrive at my own individual goal, then I have functioned as a useful member of my society.

Now people who have lived a number of years under Communist domination would hesitate to say this. They have been made aware of the "laws of historical necessity," laws which do not coincide with the interests of the individual, but are superimposed on these, making each man act at times against his social interests. They consider that when individuals have suffered under dire conditions for a long time, a new, brighter social epoch is ushered in, preceded by a violent revo-

lution and followed by a difficult period of transition. This is a law of
the dialectical evolution of society: the many quantitative failures
accumulated in the old regime are transformed into an entirely new
quality when a given point is reached. It is the purpose of the avant-
garde of the progressive layer of the population to help this process
come about by consciously preparing the social masses. Once the new
phase has arrived the duty of this elite is to carry society through the
period of transition, protecting it from the manifold dangers besetting
the way, until the dream has been consummated and man becomes
free in the ultimate phase of social evolution: Communist society,
the apex of all history.[1]

The Communist idea is undoubtedly attractive and for more than
one reason. It foresees an existence free from troubles and difficulties.
It claims that this existence is an inevitable resultant of the trouble-
some and difficult present, assures all doubters of the infallibility of
the prediction (it is "scientific") and calls for cooperation in the best
spirit of team effort. It lets the masses understand that their somewhat
low level of education and physical or intellectual skill does not make
them any less good and useful than the most accomplished and
brilliant member of high society, but makes them if anything rather
better: they are workers, and the builders of the future, while undue
brilliance and social standing are suspect of egocentricity, and hence
of an anti-social attitude. The Communist idea holds that not individual
accomplishment, but willingness to work and undeviating faith in the
scientific knowledge of the Communist Party, make men into the true
builders of Communist society. The major element in the life of all
persons is their public function, that function determines their individuality, and eventually makes all fenced-off private spheres of life
overt, socialized. While few people today are ready to accept the full
subordination of their individuality to their public function, few are
inclined to resist the pleasing idea that not qualification and ability
determine value and position, but work and faith.

---

[1] The tremendous differential between actual experience and Communist utopia
has been a major cause of the adoption of the dialectical law of the transition from
quantity to quality: by this law the differential could be seen as a positive sign of the
inevitable coming of Communist society. Where Communists are in control the differential is reduced (theoretically at least) by the society setting out on the road to
Communism. In practice, however, the differential is still large, since actual social experience
in most Communist countries is far from having reached or even approached the standard of
life obtaining in the utopian, truly Communist society. Hence the present is still very much
part of a dialectical process leading to the ultimate (and happily inevitable) state of perfect
freedom through the "non-antagonistic" contradictions of Socialist construction.

The Communist idea appears attractive enough to transform the idea of society of the majority of all people where the ideology is propagated. The idea of Communist society is contained in the teaching of Histomat. Histomat is coupled, however, with Diamat. Although the direct deduction of Histomat from Diamat practiced under Stalin is now reexamined and instead of the feasibility of full deduction their *coincidence* is posited, there is an organic nexus between the two doctrines, and this nexus is effectively propagated. Whatever effect Histomat achieves, it is restricted to influencing the individual's idea of society. The effect of Diamat, on the other hand, is felt on the individual's general *Weltanschauung* as well. As long as there is no contradiction between the two doctrines, the effect of one does not reduce the effect of the other. As not only is there no contradiction, but a general agreement prevails between the doctrines, the acceptance of one reinforces the arguments of the other. Diamat uses the same laws in its view of general reality as Histomat employs to interpret history; as a matter of fact one doctrine is capable of accounting for the other: Diamat for Histomat by deduction (although such a procedure is evidently forced), and Histomat for Diamat by induction. The latter would be scientifically illogical and is never attempted. It is sufficient to note, however, that it was nevertheless this procedure that played the major role in the creation of Diamat (as previously discussed).

The main tool of the ideology is undoubtedly Histomat. The purpose of the ideology is to transform the idea the widest masses entertain of society, and to make it accord with the Communist idea. The purpose of Diamat is a much wider one: it is to transform the *Weltanschauung* of the people to harmonize with the ontological structure of the Communist idea of society. Now of primary importance is the adoption of the idea of society. That idea gave rise to the political programme of the Communist Parties, and the adoption of that idea by the people is to make the Party programme acceptable. If both the idea of society and actual social experience is shared by all, and the idea transcends experience, then common action will be undertaken to reduce the differential: the action programme of the Party can thus find popular support. The adoption of the Communist *Weltanschauung* is of secondary importance as far as the immediate future is concerned. It takes on major significance only when long range plans are considered: the Communist *Weltanschauung* is to guarantee the effective refutation and elimination of all revisionistic tendencies coming from intellectual sources. We must consider that the majority of the people do not systematize their conception of reality, and do not require that their outlook on nature be concordant with their idea of society. Many of the intellectuals, however, (while as a class always a minority) do require such a systematic integration. Should they attempt to account for society in terms of an unbiased conception of nature, they would be tempted to reexamine their belief in Communist society. For such an eventuality a full scale theoretical structure must be at hand to prevent discrepancies from developing between the objective norms of science and the subjective norms of Marxism. Since the view of social processes is dogmatized by the assertion that Communist society is the apex of all evolution in our experience, the interpretation of general reality must be adapted to fit the interpretation of history. This is the task of Diamat. By "discovering" dialectics in all natural phenomena, and positing the materiality of the world, Diamat seeks to establish a fitting *Weltanschauung* for the Communist idea of society. Insofar as the philosophical evaluation of most natural process-es leaves room for the introduction of alternatives, and since of the alternatives only one is presented as positive, and the others (if mentio-ned at all) as negative, a scientific and intellectual atmosphere can be created that tends to accord with the political programme of the Party.

On a much wider popular level, the tenets of Diamat serve to ac-centuate the general interconnectedness of things and the fact that all things are products of dynamic processes. Hence they nourish the belief that man is the product of his manifold relations to society and is determined by social processes. The predominantly subjective evaluation of all processes thus appears to be justified, notwith-standing the circularity of the argument.[1] The result is the gradual accentuation of a subjective mode of comprehending societal reality, and may lead to the predominance of existential concepts in the people's *Weltanschauung*.

We must also take into consideration that the ideological campaign is tuned to the capacity of the average person to absorb its premisses. Where the general orientation of the nation's representative political thinking is distinctly individualistic, there the initial presentation of the ideology is geared to pull popular thought back from thinking exclusively in terms of private interests. The ultimate social ideal is camouflaged by democratic principles, the more radical ideas are

---

[1] The theory proves, and is proven by its own view of social reality, consequently all proofs involve premisses which assume the final postulates.

withheld for the time being and are only unfolded as the terrain matures and becomes more capable of absorbing collectivism.[1] A bourgeois democracy with a marked progressive content is held to be the initial step in the transformation of a nation from capitalism to socialism (even where capitalism as such did not exist, or was not predominant), to be followed by the more advanced phase of People's Democracy, and eventually by Socialism. Communism is envisaged at this time only for Soviet Russia, although it is kept as an inevitable historical necessity in abeyance for all other countries as well.

Throughout the process practice is made to reinforce theory. The nationalization of industry and the collectivization of land is proclaimed to be urgent necessities regardless whether they are or not, and thus the fruits of these practices can be praised as having saved the nation from economic ruin and the people from the ruthless exploitation of heartless capitalists and landowners. The political programme provides a "splendid confirmation" of the theory through the use of totalitarian measures. The effect on popular thought is a reinforcement of the correctness of the idea of society, and by implication, of the Communist *Weltanschauung* as well. The widest social strata are drawn into the problematic of collective existence and made aware of the benefits a holistic, planified reorganization of the social structure can reap for them. The social consciousness is gradually moulded along the lines prescribed by the theory: a specific organization of collective endeavour takes on primacy, thereby certain functions appear progressive and others reactionary, and the persons engaged in fulfilling these functions are correspondingly identified as inherently progressive or reactionary – good or bad in the ethical scale of values. Insofar as any person comes to think in these terms, his historical consciousness has been awakened. The concept of the proletariat loses much of its narrowness in the process: it gradually becomes applicable to all workers (i.e. all who work for a living) and we meet such phrases in ideological literature as the "working peasantry" and the "working, historically conscious intelligentsia."

In conclusion we must take into account that the introduction of Communism always involves large scale upheavals in the life of a society, and is accompanied by the spirit of rebuilding zeal, coupled with the sustaining optimism of such undertakings. Thus, temporarily

---

[1] As early as the 1920s Lenin declared that the masses must never be made familiar with ultimate goals (the "strategy") for this may turn them against the Communist cause; only the immediate projects (the "tactics") must be communicated to them.

at least, the attractive image of the future can substitute for the difficulties of the present, and the Communist idea of society may overshadow more realistic appraisals of the societal situation.

The Second Phase

The optimistic enthusiasm characterizing the first phase in the evolution of popular political thought under Soviet rule gradually erodes, and gives place to more sober estimates of social processes in the minds of the people. A future which is slow in transforming into reality counterbalances the ideological injections of Party head-quarters citing the "Classics", and backing their forecasts with statistical "facts." In addition to a growing scepticism, the emergence of a major area of conflict between the Party and the local population (in all nations but Russia) aggravates the growing variance between the ideology and the course taken by the people's political thinking. The problem is *nationalism*. This problem does not arise in the first phase (at least it has not arisen sofar in the case of the Satellites) owing to the injunctions of Lenin that the analysis of social problems requires that the problem be placed "within its specific historical framework and then, if the problem concerns one particular country (for example, the national programme for that country), to take account of the concrete particular traits distinguishing that country.." [1] Certainly Stalin, who had a major share in working out the original nationalist question of the Bolsheviks, adopted this attitude, and placed emphasis on his dedication to the reconstruction of independent states in Eastern Europe, asserting that the Soviet Union regards them as allies, and wished to entertain "friendly" relations with these sovereign political structures. The policy outlined in the recent Third Programme of the CPSU strikes an identical note. How is this com-patible, then, with the internationalism of the Communist world movement, and its slogan "workers of all countries, unite"? The answer lies in dialectics – as usual. The concept of nationalism is dialectical: until a certain point it has a general democratic content, thereafter it changes and acquires a bourgeois content. To understand the true nature of this transformation we must consider that the nationalist movement of a country *not* under Soviet rule (i.e. a country "oppressed by exploiters") has a "generally democratic element directed against oppression, and Communists support it because they

---

[1] Quoted by Z. Brezinski, in *The Soviet Bloc*. ch. 2.

consider it historically justified at a given stage." [1] But "Marxists-Leninists draw a distinction between the nationalism of the oppressed nations and that of the oppressor nations." [2] When a state lands in the Soviet sphere of power it is no longer oppressed, consequently its nationalism becomes reactionary in character.

The dialectics of the nationality question have very solid pragmatic foundations. The nationalism of a people is exploited by Communists as long as it is directed against the current (non- or anti-Communist) regime. Should Communists be able to take over, however, nationalism becomes a source of disunity in the Socialist system, and is predicated "reactionary," "bourgeois" and treated accordingly. As long as nationalism serves to cement Communist power in a country (this has been the case in Eastern Europe also), Communists are its most ardent champions. Indeed, as Brezinski says, "the reconstruction and maintenance of independent statehood was one of the chief planks in all Communist programmes in Eastern Europe." [3] Once the Communist elements have consolidated their power in a given nation, their main task appears to be to reevaluate local nationalism, and to fight it with the tenets of the ideology, as well as with all measures available to a centralized police state. Nationalism becomes a major source of conflict between the Party and the broad masses of each country (outside Russia itself). The reason for the conflict lies ultimately with the incompatibility of the ideological and the domestic political goals. We must consider that Communism has two major components: Marxist-Leninist ideology, and a specific political programme. The leadership institutionalizes the ideology in order to authenticate a political programme, the results of which can be held up as the brilliant confirmation of the correctness of the theory. The delicate balance obtaining between the dogmatized ideology and dynamically evolving socio-economic and intellectual conditions influencing the correctness and desirability of the political programme is kept only by the constant extension of the ideology through new "interpretations," and the adaptation of the political programme to fit the new situation without contradicting the ideology. The balance between the ideology and the political programme would be natural and constant only if the ideology would check with the exigencies of the specific historical-social situation in each country, without ever coming into more than superficial contradiction with it. This is not the case, however.

[1] *Programme of the Communist Party of the Soviet Union*, Moscow, 1961, p. 45.
[2] *Ibid.*
[3] Z. Brezinski, *op. cit.*, p. 36

Over the past few years it has become increasingly evident that the internationalism of the ideology becomes transformed into nationalism in the political programme. While the theory proclaims the full coincidence of the interests of each single nation with the interests of humanity as a whole, and in the case of the "progressive" nations, posits the coincidence of the good of every Socialist country with the good of the Soviet bloc, the actual application of the ideology, through the institutions it builds and the programmes it proposes, becomes bogged down in domestic issues and problems the solution of which poses the dilemma of the desirability of internationalism as the long-range strategy, or nationalism as the immediately effective tactic. The dilemma is that, of *ideology or power*. The ideology, as the theory of Socialist-Communist construction, posits the unconditional coincidence of the interests of all nations with the interests of Communism. Implicit in the equation is the role of Moscow: as the oldest, most powerful and most experienced progressive state, it is the natural leader of the historical epoch of the transition from Capitalism to Communism. Thus Moscow, as the leader of the fight for progress is to exercise undisputed power over all nations, for the long range goal of the Soviet leadership appears to be world domination by means of the Marxist-Leninist ideology. The theory of the coincidence of national and international interests serves this goal by cementing Soviet power through the continued use of nationalist sentiments. As long as nationalist feeling supports the Soviet cause it is identical with proletarian internationalism; when it conflicts with it, it becomes reactionary. (It should be noted in this context that internationalism itself is progressive only when it is led by a Marxist-Leninist party, otherwise it is "cosmopolitanism", a reactionary movement.)

Would practice substantiate the theory, and the interests of the Communist movement truly check with the national goals of each people, than no "national roads to Socialism" would be needed. These national roads are a fact, however, and have been endorsed by such dedicated Communists as Mao, Tito, Gomulka, Nagy, to mention only a few. The "national roads" are Marxist roads, nevertheless. They are proposed by sincere Communists, and insofar as they find a favourable echo among the masses, are also supported by people who think in Marxist categories. By the time nationalism appears on the scene as a reactionary force, it is a source of diversity among dedicated Communists: the dispute is centred on the correct application of Marxist principles, and not on the question of whether to apply it or not. If we take the local Communist Parties as the executors of the Kremlin's directives, and the representative masses of a country as patriotic adherents of the Marxian idea of society, then the national roads represent an immanent critique *by* the people *of* the Party. To arrive at this conclusion we must assume (a) that the first phase in the evolution of popular political thought under Communist rule is already concluded (the Communist idea of society is accepted by the majority), (b) that the political programme of Soviet bloc countries is directed by Moscow and is thus guided by the consideration of Soviet bloc interests, rather than by the immediate needs of the national scene.[1] The infiltration of the Communist idea of society in the social consciousness results in a wide differential between the people's idea of society and their actual social experience, and the impetus for the support of political action programmes is provided by this differential.

As a result the prime motivation of political action is the immediate interest of the nation, rather than the interest of the Communist movement as a whole. Should the interests of the international movement coincide with what the people take to be the proper interest of their nation, there is no reason to suppose that international interests would be rejected – on the contrary, they would provide further impetus to the support of a given programme. Whenever these interests conflict, however, popular support is usually lent to those project which back national interests, and projects of international scope are opposed proportionately to their incompatibility with the evident good of the nation. In this discussion the term "nation" has been given a primary importance, requiring now its definition in more precise terms. A nation, when used in the context wherein wide masses use it, and in the sense in which it can give rise to spontaneous feelings of identification by individuals, must be that sphere of social experience which is given by the immediate network of existential relations. A nation is thus the group or collectivity which shares a pattern of experience, has a unified system of laws, customs, history, and perhaps (though not necessarily) one exclusive language. In this definition a "nation" comes close to being equated with "state," since given sufficient time, several nationalities united into one constituted state become forged into a measure of unity which tends to replace previous divisions, and make multination states into one united nation in the

---

[1] If and when the local Party secedes from Moscow's direct control, it echoes the people's immanent critique (subject to political expediency), but directed at the CPSU. To that extent ideological diversity becomes institutionalized.

eyes of the majority. (Such has been the case in the USSR, in Yugoslavia, Italy, Germany, Chechoslovakia, to mention only a few.)
Internal division may be apparent for a relatively long time following
organizational unification; however, diversity tends to disappear
when the people have to choose between domestic and truly "foreign"
interests. Common interests and common adversaries forge a unity
in political thinking, in which multination states equal historically
formed single nations. Thus for the evolution of political thought
under Communism federal state-structures function as one nation,
and the conflict between national and international interests treats
even federated states as a unity.

Since the Socialist bloc states are not federated, (outside of the
USSR) but each nation is permitted to keep its original, ostensibly
autonomous state structure, the internationalist goals of the movement
as a whole involve, in the eyes of the people, the subordination of
national interests for the good of *foreign* nations. Despite of nationalist
resistence, Communism functions for the Moscow leadership as a tool
for power-political ends, and thus there is no hesitation in suppressing
nationalism whenever it is politically possible and expedient. The local
Communist Parties institutionalize internationalist aims in the body
of each nation, and hope to find support for their programme by
equating the good of the nation with the good of the movement as a
whole. When this equation breaks down (as it is eventually bound
to do), two distinct factions develop: the Party leadership backed by
the *apparatchiki*, following the internationalist (Moscow directed)
line; and the wide masses embracing members of all economic and
culture groups, who are motivated by patriotic, nationalist political
ambitions. Thus the characteristic feature of this phase is the developing dichotomy of the national scene, consisting in one part of an
official political line, and in another of popular, and no longer institutionalized political thinking. The conflict between them involves
most of all questions of means, for the end has been accepted by the
representative majority of both factions as the Communist idea of
society.

Thus, if the interests of the nation would truly coincide with the
interests of the Communist system, these factions would neither
develop nor come into opposition. However, the imperialistic goals
set by the Kremlin leaders involve interference with the organization
of the nations of the Socialist bloc, and lead to national interests being
shortchanged. National interests are shortchanged for power-political

goals to some extent even in Russia, despite the fact that there at least, the Kremlin's and the people's interests would appear to coincide. While such a coincidence is true of several areas of Russian national interest, the exigencies of international ideological politics do not fully and always correspond to the requirements of Russia's optimum welfare.[1] Insistence on measures which serve the Kremlin's foreign policy renders its domestic programme less satisfactory for the population than a nationalist application of Communist principles would. This disparity between national and ideo-political goals is naturally much more flagrant in the Satellites. There the Communist international system, through the agency of the local Communist Party, comes to represent a foreign power in the eyes of the local population. That aspect of Marxism-Leninism which was most of all Lenin's contribution, namely the centralized Communist international Party organization, comes ever more into conflict with the national interests of Communist satellites. Consequently the internationalist aspect of the integral doctrine comes to be resented and, at times, violently hated by the people of the Socialist bloc. Thus it could come about that the word "Communist" is the object of criticism, while the ideas of Communism are at the same time embraced and supported. The ideas of Communist *theory* are adopted by and effectively present in, the political thinking of the people (given sufficient exposure to the ideology) while the Communist *system* is excluded from it proportionately to the time spent under Soviet domination. The schism between theory and system thus takes on ever greater dimensions, and can, if unchecked, produce spontaneous revolts. These revolts, if and when they take place, are not anti-Communist revolutions, when by "Communist" we understand a person who has adopted Histomat's idea of society and Diamat's conception of reality. They are anti-Communist revolutions, however, when we take as "Communist" the person who faithfully supports the Communist Party organization, and its political programme. It is imperative therefore, to keep the Communist theory and the system distinct when analysing the political situation under Soviet rule: the theory gives rise to wide-spread national-collectivist political convictions, while the system is accepted and applied only by the Party *apparatchiki*. The basic cause of the

[1] The Kremlin's dilemma is the consideration that "the divorce of Communist ideology from Soviet national interest would not strengthen the ideology within the USSR, while their continued linkage is likely to breed resentment and weaken that ideology elsewhere." Z. Brezinski, *Communist Ideology and International Affairs*, Conflict Resolution, Sept. 1960. p. 283.

domestic troubles of the Socialist bloc on the ideological level in the second phase is due mainly to the failure of the international system to satisfy the interests close to the hearts of the people while at the same time offering a theory which could provide, in a national application, a much higher level of satisfaction. Since the majority comes to think along the lines proposed by the theory, people can exercise an immanent critique on its application. The basic collectivist thought developed by Marx and propagated at full ideological pressure by the Communist Parties, furnishes concepts and ideas in light of which the actual practice of the Party appears not only to be less than optimum, but actually *wrong*. The criticism of the Party by the people represents the criticism of the system by means of the theory. Since the Communist international system is the means of exercising centralized control over the entire Socialist bloc, the criticism of the system, even if done by otherwise sincere Communists, is in no way less, but rather more dangerous to the Kremlin's designs than criticism from the opposite camp. To counteract such criticisms the Kremlin (a) emphasizes the international character of the Communist movement, and (b) asserts that the Marxist-Leninist ideology and the Communist international system are effective only conjointly.[1]

Notwithstanding the internationalism of Communist theory and politics, the fact remains, however, that in most countries of the Socialist bloc the system is not accepted as part of the theory and thus a dichotomy of the Communist ideology results. The second phase in the evolution of political thought under Communist rule shows that ideology can divide rather than unite, notwithstanding the success of the first phase in lending a common idea of society to the representative

---

[1] Of the many texts dealing with these questions the following are representative: "The line of socialist construction in isolation, detached from the world community ot socialist countries is theoretically untenable because it conflicts with the objective laws governing the development of socialist society." (Programme of the CPSU, 1961) "The consolidation of the socialist countries in a single camp, its increasing unity and steadily growing strength ensures the complete victory of Socialism and Communism within the framework of the system as a whole." (*Ibid.*) "The Marxist-Leninist Parties consider internationalism as an essential constitutive component of their ideology and their politics. Without internationalism, without the efforts of the workers of all countries, it is impossible to defeat world bourgeoisie and to construct the new society." (*Osnovi Marksizma-Leninizma*, 11.4.) These recent texts are based on the theses of Marx and Engels: "Workers of all countries unite" and are supported by the explicit formulations of Lenin: "The socialist movement cannot be victorious within the old framework of the fatherland. It creates new, higher forms of human life under which the demands and progressive tendencies of the labouring masses of all nationalities will be fully satisfied in an international unity, while the present national partitions are destroyed." (Lenin, *Položenie i zadachi sosialističeskogo internationala* (*Nov. 1. 1914*) *Sočineniya*, Vol. xviii, p. 70)

majority of the people of the Soviet bloc.[1] Krushchev warned not without reason that to allow full independence to the various Communist Parties "would lead the Communist and Workers' Parties to contradictory action and, in the final count, to disagreement".[2]

The Third Phase

The first phase in the evolution of political thought in the Soviet bloc belongs to the past. The second phase is actually taking place, while the third phase is still of the future. Nevertheless, it is not mere fortune telling in which we indulge here, when we attempt to outline the major characteristics of the third phase. There are concrete signs of it available for study today, signs which are most likely the forerunners of a more powerful movement. These are the signs of a beginning erosion of the ontological principle of the idea of Communist society. While revisionism directed against the system through the reinterpretation of the theory represents an immanent critique, and is thus an internal affair of the Socialist bloc, the erosion of the ontological principle signifies the *rapprochement* of the ontological structure of Marxist-Leninist collectivism and democratic individualism, and thus involves the conflict of the contemporary power blocs. *Transcendental* criticism of Communism originates from within the ranks of Marxist-Leninists, moulds the theory and takes greater distance from its extreme unilateral point of view. In proposing the thesis that Marxist-Leninist ideology has the power to transform a nation's political thinking from an essentially individualist to an essentially collectivist pattern, we have not assumed that it also has the power to *keep* political thought collectivist under changing conditions and through several generations. It is this problem that we shall analyse here.

Communism is oldest in the USSR: there the present generation grew up already in a collectivist climate. In the other countries of the Socialist bloc the elder generation has grown up under individualism, and (aside from the numerically small group of pre-war Communists) became acquainted with collectivist thought first-hand only in 1945, or even later. Consequently it is only in the Soviet Union that the greater part of the population has no basis of comparison between life in a collectivist and in an individualist society. Only personal

---

[1] Ideological diversity on the popular and spontaneous level is illustrated by our documentation of a case of nationalist revisionism, cf. pp. 111–140. Second-phase diversity on the *institutionalized* level is evident behind the politics of all inter-Party disputes (e.g. Yugoslavia, Albania, China).

[2] *Pravda*, June 4, 1958.

experience could serve for comparison; Communist ideology being totalitarian, filters all indirect knowledge of individualism through the optic of historical materialism. The majority of the people in the USSR are thus fully under the influence of the ideas of Communism and of the intellectual and cultural atmosphere created by the Communist ideology, knowing no other mode of life or mode of thinking except as reactionary, either feudalistic or bourgeois, but always as that of a declining and doomed order. The average citizen is presented with the collectivist climate of the USSR without having a basis of comparison or having any criteria for judgments of his own. As a consequence the psychological atmosphere of the Soviet Union can achieve its maximum effect, not fearing recollections of other, perhaps more attractive, cultural and intellectual climates.

The atmosphere of collectivism is characterized by the constant affirmation of the primacy of the group and its interests over that of the individual, focusing attention thereby on the problems and importance of correct social organization, and the team effort necessary for realizing it. Collectivism deals with the relational determination of the person, it cognizes societal reality subjectively, in terms of the problems posed and resolved by relational human existence. This view of society is basic to the individual whose social existence is acutely problematic. In a non-partisan social climate, however, the definition of just what kind of problems can be designated "acute" must take into consideration the intellectual capacities of the person. A modest intellect can seldom penetrate beyond the subjective mode of comprehension in assessing his environment, while a highly developed man is likely to concentrate on the problems of his social existence only as long as these problems prevent him from tackling other, more objective areas of inquiry. Should the existential problematic of an advanced intellectual ease, and should the intellectual climate of his society be free from strong and purposive bias, he is likely to comprehend his problems more objectively, using the subjective mode of evaluation and comprehension only when dealing with objects and relations vitally involving his personal well-being. In a Communist climate, on the other hand, all things and all relations are evaluated subjectively, following the Marxian formulation of practice as the proof of knowledge, and the good of man as the criterion for the desirability of practical activity. It follows then that knowledge in a Communist society represents the comprehension of the environment in the context of its effect upon man, more precisely upon the collectivity, as determinant of men. The problem of keeping popular political thought Communist, and preserving the spirit of partisanship for dialectical and historical materialism, is the problem of preventing individuals from evaluating and comprehending societal and general reality in unbiased, objective terms. Normally, objective thinking is likely to develop when the standard of existence for the intellectual class as a whole is sufficiently elevated to free the thinkers from involvement in problems of basic survival, permitting them to detach their view of reality from the subjective context of need. The spread of this kind of comprehension in society would bring about the downfall of the authority of dialectical and historical materialism. By creating a partisan, biased climate, the CPSU attempts to counteract this development. The Party does this by upholding all achievements of the USSR and the Communist movement as a direct confirmation of Marxism-Leninism, and by continuing large scale social construction toward a glorious future. Since the present and the future require unselfish, collective effort, and the past has "confirmed" the correctness of the plans for the future, the average person feels himself vitally involved in the fate and politics of his country. The Communist system can thus prevent the average Soviet citizen from starting objective, unbiased trains of thought himself. Every public media, from the Party's Central Committee and the Supreme Soviet, to the council of the smallest isolated kolkhoz, from Pravda to local Party organs, Radio and Television, are made to serve the task of keeping alive the Socialist team-spirit, according to which all individuals work and exist primarily for the benefit of their local organization, the organization works and exists for the good of the nation, and the nation works, fights and exists for the good of the Socialist world system – and that system incorporates the highest achievement and ultimate hope of all mankind; the entire process being directed and supervised by the Communist Parties, the faithful followers of the great teachers of the world-proletariat Marx, Engels and Lenin. Hence in the final analysis every Soviet citizen is seen to work and exist for the good of all mankind, the effectiveness of his existence being guaranteed by the infallible teachings of Marxism-Leninism. In a climate where each man is considered a benefactor of humanity by virtue of his work, the importance of social existence is constantly emphasized, and subordination of concepts of individual being comes naturally. Any potential slackening of interest in the great team-effort is counterbalanced by new "gigantic" projects, comprising not only economic multi-year plans and production quotas, but also the construction of Soviet society as a whole. The party adopted the plan for building Socialism in 1919 (the second Programme of the CPSU) and considers this task to have been completed. It now goes on to plan the building of Communist society (outlined in the Third Programme of the CPSU, adopted in 1961) without slackening the pace. This construction (making the USSR the first country in the world to reach the highest form of social existence, according to Marxism-Leninism) is to take twenty years. The unquestioning loyalty of all Soviet people is requested to build and safeguard the cause of Communism both inside and outside the USSR.

The collectivist spirit dominates also Soviet education. From the very first day a child goes to school, he is treated as the member of a group (his class, or even the row in which he sits) rather than as an individual. The group is responsible for each member, and it is up to the group or its chosen spokesman to deal with all its problems, be it a lazy student or a difficult professor. The collective spirit of school is, of course, unfavourably affected by home life. Within his family the child is treated as an individual; his particular desires and specific characteristics are taken into account as the properties of a single, individual person. Hence homelife tends to act as a brake on the gradual submersion of the incompatible features of the child's individuality with the features and position of his group. It is significant of the consciousness of the importance of these factors by the Soviet leadership that they back a highly intensified programme for the transformation of the school system from day- to boarding-schools. Boarding-schools provide the best form of education under conditions obtaining during the building of Communism, declared the Central Committee in announcing its seven year plan in 1959.

Thus from earliest childhood all through adult life to old age, the contemporary Soviet citizen spends his days in a consciously collectivist atmosphere, designed to emphasize the secondary importance of the individual in relation to his group. Consequently the Soviet Union's relatively elevated, and now stabilizing standard of existence is constantly infused with the collectivist spirit of great spontaneous national movements. The collectivism of the Marxist-Leninist theory is reinforced by a daily pattern of experience which "substantiates" the theory.

The expansion and increasing power of the Socialist international system is upheld as the confirmation of the validity of the effort as a whole, while technological victories in the space and arms race, in production capacities, the success of Soviet artists and sports figures are publicized as proof of the effectiveness of the doctrine with respect to specific fields. The success of each person is the success of the ideology, and the power of the system as a whole is its confirmation.

The climate created by such measures is not conducive to pessimism, nor to the abandonment of the line of action adopted so far. Prospects for the erosion of the ontological principle of the Communist idea of society are dim when we consider the masses in the immediate and near future. In taking the long-range view, however, the picture changes.

The role of the Soviet Union as a world power and contender to world leadership necessitates the encouragement of maximum effort in all fields relevant to power and glory. A new type of thinking must be developed among the members of the new generation, a type of thinking which is in direct opposition with the traditional Russian mode of thought and its leaning toward mysticism, utopia, and the acceptance of theoretical, unverifiable, but pleasantly harmonious and elegant explanations of general reality. There is no doubt that the traditional leaning to such thinking has played a major role in the relatively smooth transplantation of Marxism from Germany to Russia. This mentality, which is so conducive to the acceptance of the ideology, is unfit to deal with the complex problems of modern technological and scientific research. Technological-scientific research is vitally important for Soviet Russia as a great power; and for progress in these domains, undogmatic, creative thinking is a precondition.

By assuming that Marx, Engels and Lenin have said the last word about natural phenomena, scientific and technological progress would come to a standstill. The problem is much more then, how to do objective research, and interpret the results by finding new meanings in the aging texts. Evidently, this is not always possible. As a result there is a changing relationship between researchers and Party theoreticians, aided by the always increasing importance attributed to scientists and technicians in Soviet society. This relationship lends greater authority to the investigators, and makes for their increasing independence from ideological control. The dilemma of *ideology, or power* is an acute one not only in the second, but also in the third phase of the evolution of political thought under Communism. In this phase the alternatives are (a) full maintenance of the ideology, at the risk of falling behind in the technological and armament race, or (b) proceeding full speed ahead in all fields of research, and perhaps compromising the ideology's authority in the process.

The new technological elite of the USSR is raised for a specific purpose – the winning of the great race with the capitalist world through the development of Soviet supremacy in all civil and military fields, by all technological and scientific means capable of aiding production and striking capacity. In fulfilling its function the new elite is gradually emancipated from ideological pressures and clothed with a novel authority of its own. The scientifically and technologically highly trained specialist has no major reason to use his knowledge to oppose Soviet internationalism by taking a nationalist attitude, since much of the internationalist goals of the Kremlin coincide with national interests – those that do not, are not sufficiently strong to turn the technological-scientific elite as a class, against the Party.[1]

The friction between the new class and the CPSU is more likely to develop on another plane instead: on the level of theoretical thought. The Party assumes a fully partisan position with respect to the tenets of dialectical and historical materialism, not tolerating the influence of any but the most unavoidable and incorrigible contradictions to reach the theoretical edifice. The Marxist-Leninist view of social as well as natural processes is held to be absolutely valid by the Party leadership; while a true scientific spirit, capable of leading to technolo-gical-scientific progress, *must* keep an open mind concerning the still unexplored facets of empirical experience.

The unbiased implications of modern physics, for example, threaten the Communist view of reality, since the western scientist's world of four-dimensional time-space coordinates does not obey dialectical laws of evolution and is, as far as experiential evidence can show, finite, rather than infinite. The conclusions of the western scientist (that the processes of evolution are not identical with the Hegelian notion of dialectics, and that the world is finite, having an undefined substance capable of being accounted for either as waves or particles) is unacceptable to Communism: these implications contradict not only the dialectical materialist *Weltanschauung*, but also the premisses which are to make socialist construction truly "scientific." While the

[1] The new technological-scientific elite is not identical with the traditional Russian in-telligentsia. Indeed, as Seton-Watson says, "The intelligentsia as a separate political and social group has ceased to exist and it has been incorporated in the state bourgeoisie, to which its name has been arbitrarily given." (Hugh Seton-Watson, "The Role of the Intelligentsia", *Survey*, August 1962.) Both the mentality and the social position of the new class differ from that of the traditional intelligentsia of Russian society.

unbiased implications of all branches of natural science manifest points of divergence from Diamat, the conflict is most acute in physics, and not only because modern physics does not deal with matter as a category, and slights dialectics in its views of evolution, but because supremacy in nuclear and astro-physics is a major component of the Communist-Capitalist world contest, and supremacy depends on good progress in research through the correct approach and evaluation of the problems.[1] But the conflict of modern thought and aging doctrines is felt in the stronghold of the Soviet ideology, in Marxist-Leninist philosophy itself.

According to the observations of western specialists in Soviet philosophy, recent Soviet literature in the field has shown a general modification in form as well as in content, which might be taken to augur a coming transformation. The following are particularly note-worthy: (i) the lessening of "deductivism" – meaning a less frequent use of the accepted Soviet custom of substantiating a premiss by deducing it from a statement by one of the "Classics" (Marx, Engels, Lenin, and until recently, Stalin); (ii) the decrease of "quotatology" in recent Soviet philosophy (there has been somewhat less use made of direct

---

[1] S. Müller-Markus lists the external signs of the conflict between Diamat and natural science in his study "Sowjetphilosophie in der Krise" (*Schweitzer Monatshefte*, July 1962) as follows:

December 1948: Conference on the ideological problems of Astronomy in Leningrad: Refutation of the theory of cosmic expansion.

1951–55: Discussion about relativity theory: refutation of the Einstein thesis.

1955: official acknowledgment of relativity theory.

1952: "The Philosophic Problems of Modern Physics" (a collective study of the Soviet Academy of Science): sharp attacks on modern physics.

March 1954: Conference on the philosophical problems of modern physics in Kiev, with the participation of leading scientists and philosophers: discussion of relativity theory and quantum indeterminism. Since 1951, yearly conference on cosmogony.

1957: acknowledgment of the Doppler-effect (and with that of the theory of cosmic expansion).

1958: All-union conference on the philosophical problems of modern natural science in Moscow: discussions on relativity theory, cosmogony, and acknowledgment of indeterminism in quantum mechanics by the leading Soviet physicist Fok.

1959: Foundation of a scientific council of the Academy of Science for the philosophical problems of natural science.

1961: Foundation of a Central Office of the philosophical (methodological) Seminars of the Academy of Science. (There are 56 such Seminars in Moscow alone).

December 1960: Conference on the philosophical problems of physics in Moscow University.

February 1961: Conference on Positivism in Moscow University.

January 1961: Conference on Diamat as foundation of modern science in Kiev.

It is also worthy of note that the Chinese attempt at scientific objectivism, introduced in 1956 by the words of Ch'ien Chün-jui (then deputy director of the second office of the State Council) "to raise the level of our science and technology, we must, in matters of scholarship, thoroughly carry out the policy of free discussion and 'letting a hundred schools contend'" was saved from disaster for the regime in May, 1957 only by a hard hitting "anti-Rightist" campaign. cf. Th. H. E. Chen, *Thought Reform of the Chinese Intellectuals*, Hong Kong, 1960, pp. 117ff.

quotations from classical texts); (iii) increased tolerance of individual viewpoints, reaching at times to an overt or implied contradiction of a postulate of one of the Classics (usually Engels, though to some degree Lenin as well) always provided the postulate is supported by a proposition of another, or preferably the same Classic; (iv) the "declassification" of some fields of inquiry from the zone where ideological dogmatism holds absolute sway (among these mention should be made particularly of formal logic and cybernetics, as well as of Einsteinian physics and mathematical logic); (v) a growing tendency to "historicize" entire works by the Classics, regarding them as historical moments in the evolution of Diamat and Histomat, rather than as unconditionally valid in the immediate meaning of the propositions (sofar only Engels' *Dialectics of Nature* is so treated, although rumours hold that this is the likely fate of Lenin's *Materialism and Empiriocriticism* as well).[1]

Soviet (and Satellite) philosophy is beset not only by problems posed by science, but also by the problems arising out of the incompatibility of collectivism, as a central principle of the theoretical structure, with all efforts to explicate the attributes, values, and characteristics of the individual as such.[2] The periodic crises of Communist philosophy, resulting in purges of the academic cadres under the guise of weeding out revisionists, are due in large part to the attempts of sincere but shortsighted scholars to develop a "Marxist anthropology" "Marxist ethics" "Marxist sociology" "Marxist psychology" and similar specialized inquiries into the nature of the individual and his problems in a context other than that provided by the optic of Histomat, which reduces, in the end, to an ultimate determination of the individual by the relations of production obtaining in the given society. It is evident that, following the tenets of Histomat neither of the above disciplines have a *raison d'être* as specialized inquiries, for if the individual is the product of his society then the problems of the individual must be located and treated on the level of the collectivity, rather

---

[1] The above points have been compiled by the author at a recent meeting of the Institute of East-European Studies at the University of Fribourg (Switzerland). For an integral treatment of contemporary Soviet philosophy see the *Sovietica* series of the Institute, as well as G. Wetter, *Der Dialektische Materialismus*, and *Sowjetideologie heute*, I. M. Bochenski, *Der Sowjetrussische Dialektische Materialismus*, and Bochenski-Niemeyer (eds.) *Handbuch des Weltkommunismus*.

[2] A. Buchholz terms the questions which are seriously discussed in the West but not in Soviet philosophy, "empty domains" of Diamat. He lists as such the question of the meaning of life; the problem of death; intuitive knowledge; and all questions of the individual and his problems. (A. Buchholz, "The Ideological East-West Conflict," *Studies in Soviet Thought*, Volume I.)

than looking for values, qualities and characteristics in the individual himself. It is becoming increasingly clear, however, that inquiries concerning the individual cannot be suppressed by purges and ideological control.[1] The development of such disciplines and their specialized methods of treating the problem of the individual, signify a spread of objectivism among the academic circles. However, through the increasing size of the educated and highly trained classes the (sofar localized) infiltration of objectivism in the Soviet idea of societal and general reality is likely to spread. Technical progress brings with it an approach to problems which often fails to check with, or is difficult to interpret in the light of, the ideology's tenets, and whenever such conflict develops, the ideology is likely to lose authority proportionately to the success of Soviet science and technology. For the time being the contested fields belong almost exclusively to the domain of Diamat. Inasmuch, however, as the authority of Histomat is dependent on the acceptance of Diamat (a dependence which current efforts to separate the two fields can do little to mitigate in the eyes of the wide public), and Diamat is subjected to increasing pressure, the "scientific" nature of Histomat's view of social processes is bound to be questioned eventually.

Marxism-Leninism, the theory of collectivism adopted and propagated by the Soviet Union, has proven to be a useful ontological principle for the elimination of the extreme social stratification obtaining under the Tsarist regime. But, in the course of time it created new conditions, and became incorporated into the *Weltanschauung* deriving from these conditions. From the continued interaction of ideology and living society a new mode of political thinking is about to arise, which will transcend both the original theory and the original thinking of the people. Although the ideology is constantly stretched to correspond to fresh situations, its creative extension has strict limitations: it cannot pass beyond collectivism. The very essence of Communism (though Communists are reluctant nowadays to admit it) lies in the assumption that the being of the individual is subordinate to his social existence, and in the belief that the collectivity determines the individual. Owing to these essential

---

[1] In current Hungarian philosophy, for example (a faithful mirror of its Soviet counterpart) major attacks have centred on Agnes Heller for her "individualist humanism" evident in her attempt to work out a system of Marxist ethics, and on Sándor Szalai for attempting to apply western sociological methods in Hungary. But notwithstanding the banning of Heller and Szalai, there is a greatly increased interest in ethics and sociology in Hungary today.

premisses, the country with the longest exposure to the Communist ideology, having developed powerful and extensive intellectual classes and accorded them privileged positions, will inevitably tend to erode belief in the correctness and power of unilateral collectivism, although countries where Communism is still new, and where intellectual classes are neither extensive nor powerful, will as yet show the zeal and faith demanded of builders of socialism. This contention is illustrated by the present Sino-Soviet ideological dispute. While the arguments of theoreticians must not be taken to faithfully explicate a nation's thinking, the theses and polemics of the Chinese leaders nevertheless evidence the confidence and enthusiasm of a people having passed through the first phase in the evolution of political thought under Communism and now entering upon the second, with its intense drives of ideological, economic, and political emancipation, just as the Soviet reaction testifies to that elite's approaching the third phase, characterized by cautious appraisals and lack of trust in the omnipotence of the ideological movement. Underneath tactical moves in the game of Communist power politics, recognizable long-range processes take their course. If these are permitted to develop during a sustained period of "peaceful co-existence" the centre of orthodox Marxism-Leninism is likely to shift to Peking, while Moscow will be pressured toward an ideological *rapprochement* with democratic individualism first by external, power-political pressures partially created, and certainly intensified by real ideological differences with China, and then also by internal, purely ideological influences emanating from the Soviet intellectual elite in the form of increasing objectivism and the consequent loss of faith in the validity of the principle of unilateral collectivism. If Communism is not threatened by an imminent revolution, it is not immune to the erosive effect of a gradual evolution either. In the long run, it is beyond the power of any system of social organization to perpetuate itself by any scheme or practice based upon the dogmatic acceptance of a unilateral ontological principle as the one and absolute truth.

III

NATIONAL REVISIONISM: A CASE HISTORY

Ever since the Bolsheviks came to power in Russia, the Kremlin's policy was to tolerate, and nominally encourage nationalism on the state level, while enforcing strict centralization on the Party level. As the local Communist Parties control the functioning of the state in each national area, this policy permitted the Kremlin to exercise effective control over the Soviet bloc while advocating at the same time the principles of national autonomy and the sovereignty of states.[1] The autonomy of a Soviet bloc country as a sovereign state means simply the local administration of the state apparatus; alone the autonomy of the Communist Party could signify the independence of the nation from Soviet rule. The Communist Parties of Yugoslavia and Red China seceded from the control of the CPSU, and could thus insure the actual, as opposed to the nominal, sovereignty of these nations. These countries have institutionalized their nationalist revisionism, and thus go their own way relatively freely. Other East European Satellites, on the other hand, are still under the yoke of Communist Kremlin-controlled dictatorship. These countries can provide the best examples of the typical development of popular political thought under Communism. Before undertaking an analysis of the spontaneous national revisionism of a Soviet dominated people, let us recall in outline the major events leading to the "Sovietization" of Eastern Europe since the end of the Second World War.

Following the Yalta Conference the formula of organization of Eastern European countries was based on the idea of "National Fronts." These were designed to unite each country and avoid the splits between rival groups and political parties which could weaken the common fight against Fascism. The greatest potential source of

[1] These tactics permit the "dialectical" manipulation of the nationality question by placing emphasis either on international unity or national diversity, as the occasion requires.

conflict lay in the opposition of pro-Western and pro-Soviet sympathies. Since the Soviet Union was one of the signatories of the treaty giving rise to these Fronts, an anti-Soviet sentiment in the organizations could not be tolerated. Yet the National Fronts rested on a primarily nationalist motivation which, in some countries was distinctly anti-Soviet, the previous regime having instilled anti-Communist feelings into the minds of the population. Thus it came about that the leaders of national resistence movements at first rejected all ideas of cooperation with Communists, in whom they saw the direct agents of the Kremlin. A powerful pressure was required to provide a semblance of cooperation between the opposing factions. Consequently the coalitions resulting from the insistence of the Great Powers had a far more delicate character in Eastern Europe than anywhere in the West: they could be maintained only through the constant intervention of the Great Powers. These interventions had a reactionary effect upon the projected national unification of the countries: instead of the new governments uniting the people under a common flag, each faction of the coalitions sought the protection of one or the other of the Powers, and thus contributed to a dissociation of the government from the national feelings and interests of the people. While the politicians searched for support in Moscow, London and Washington, the people had learned to distrust the government and regard their leaders as mere agents of foreign powers. In the meanwhile the balance of international power shifted and resulted in the increasing domination of Eastern Europe by Soviet Russia. The continued presence of the Red Army in these countries was undoubtedly the major factor in their political development. The leaders of the People's Republics did not fail to admit the importance of this influence. Mátyás Rákosi, the head of the Hungarian Communists, was among the first to acknowledge the role of the army. In the official organ of Marxism-Leninism in Hungary, he wrote that the presence of Soviet troops had condemned all serious resistance from the beginning, made a civil war impossible and in comparison with the Red Army's presence even the Party's work had but a limited importance in assuring the loyalty of the Hungarian Army.[1]

While the people of Hungary, Eastern Germany, Rumania and Poland were decidedly anti-Soviet in orientation, those of Czechoslovakia and Yugoslavia had virulent Communist streaks. In these countries Soviet politics could make use of well-organized and influential Communist Parties, could make the Soviet Union appear as the champion of Slavism and could offer various economic advantages in exchange for political influence. The political goals of the Soviets co-incided with the national aspirations of these countries to a remarkable extent: Communism could feed on national sentiment. Where the national orientation was anti-Soviet, however, the process was slower, but could nevertheless obtain an apparent success. The basic factor in this was the presence of the Red Army, insuring the cooperation of the governments. Through their cooperation ideological, economic and political programmes could be put into effect, and Communist power be built up. This much is historical fact. But the question of how far, or rather how deep, Communist power reaches in the Satellites is less evident from such facts. To examine this problem we must consider that in aiding the economic development of these countries the USSR has not satisfied their most essential requirement. The economic development of all East-European Satellites has been significant, and in some cases even spectacular. Yet not much of the benefits of this East-European "Wirtschaft-Wunder" has reached the people. The primary consideration of the Soviets in providing the conditions for economic development was the subordination of each country to the Soviet bloc as a whole. For this reason heavy industry was developed in a highly specialized manner, making the countries dependent on each other's trade, assured through the agreements of the Warsaw Pact. Consumer goods are considered secondary to heavy industrial production for this specific stage in the construction of Socialist society. Economy is thus used first of all as a means for insuring the various Satellites' dependence on the Soviet bloc, and not as the instrument for satisfying the practical demands of their people. Although consumer goods, and even certain foods were and are scarce, the importance of this factor must not be overestimated when dealing with the problem of national revisionism. The great reconstruction movement after the sufferings and privations of the second World War brought with it a remarkable disregard for the amenities and luxuries of daily life. The idea of a great national rebirth was domi-nant in the people's minds: suffering develops loyalty ties, and common redemption from common trials intensifies these sentiments. The roots of national revisionism lie in the further encouragement of national loyalties by the collectivism required for the construction and maintenance of Communist society, and in the disregard by the Communist international system of pride in national accomplishment.

The new constitutions adopted in 1945 appear to have been inspired by
a consideration of the interests of the nation as a whole: they abolished
the Monarchies, the rule of aristocracies, feudal privileges, took the
power from the hands of the great land-owners and industrialists. Yet
in practice the State institutions – parliaments, municipal councils,
rural authorities, (etc.) – were transformed into mere instruments of
propaganda, into so called "transmission organizations" after 1948,
without real power or capacity for initiative of their own. The People's
Democracies have always been presented as a special form of the
dictatorship of the proletariat; in reality, however, the nation's proletariat never exercised any real power. The working classes receive
benefits under the new Constitution (better pay, paid vacation, social
insurance, possibilities of advancement and so on), but these achievements are neutralized by a totalitarian system which takes all initiative from these "progressive" (and in fact progressing) classes, subordinating their newly-acquired pride of accomplishment to the superior achievements of a foreign power. The real danger to the Communist system is constituted by these progressing classes, trained to
higher intellectual levels and developing a "scientific" mentality able
to distinguish fact from fiction. Marxist-Leninist theory infuses the
idea of team-effort for the collective good into their minds, while
depriving them of the power to act on their own initiative. The Socialist state awakens wide nationalist forces which the strategy of the
Communist international system is always less capable of satisfying
and containing. The Party is sufficiently well organized, however, to
withstand these pressures for a considerable time. Nevertheless, the
system can and does occasionally burst wide open in spontaneous
national revolts. Such has been the case among others in Poland,
East-Germany and Hungary.

If we are to study national revisionism on the level of the wide
masses, truly representative of a nation, we must concentrate on these
outbursts, for every form of approved and institutionalized revisionism under Communist rule keeps the totalitarianism of the Party, and
cannot, for this reason, give a reliable picture of the motivation of the
movement below the leadership level. Thus for example, despite Yugoslavia having adopted a nationalist position in the Socialist camp,
claiming full autonomy for its own Communist Party, and sanctioning
revisionism in philosophical and ideological literature, the fallacy of accepting the Yugoslav Party's ideological thesis and its political programme as fully representative of the nation's political thinking becomes

evident when we take into account the occasions when the Party, under Tito's leadership calmly condemned national Communism elsewhere, for reasons of political expediency.[1] Inasmuch as any political Party adopts Marxist-Leninist principles, it acts on the assumption that the social consciousness (i.e. the actual political thinking) of the masses lags behind the course of events, and that they must therefore, be further educated to cognize social realities. As we have seen, "education" often means withholding knowledge of the real objectives, or camouflaging them under more popular principles. Nevertheless, the people of the Satellites are capable of giving expression to their own political thought, and can communicate them to the western world from time to time. One of the most flagrant occasions when a Communist ruled nation's genuine political objectives were broadcoast without totalitarian censorship was during the Hungarian uprising of 1956. The period of contact was brief (ten days in all), but it is well documented: hundreds of demands and ultimatums were printed and broadcast by rebel radios. Most of these are available for study. The problem in the case of Hungary lies not so much in gaining access to the nation's genuine political thinking (for that is granted by the documents without doubt) but rather in evaluating the evidence in the correct historical-social context. For this reason it is necessary to consider the specific influences acting upon the political thinking of the Hungarians since the great changeover at the end of World War II.

During the Horthy regime Hungary was exposed to German influences on all levels of its civilisation, from the cultural to the economic and political. It is not surprising therefore that in the last free elections held in Hungary on November 4, 1945, the freshly formed Communist Party should have polled not more than 17.11% of all votes cast, obtaining 70 seats in Parliament out of a total of 409. At the same time the petit bourgeois and nationalist Smallholders Party could obtain 59.9% of the votes and gain 245 seats in Parliament. Undoubtedly the Communist Party would not have reached even these comparatively poor results, had not the liberation from the yoke of a losing and desperate Nazi Germany been effected by the Soviet Army, tuning popular sentiment favourably toward all things Russian. It is clear, however, that in 1945 Hungary was not any more sympathetic to Communism than it has been in 1919, during the brief spell of Béla

---

[1] We are referring to Tito's condemnation of fellow national Communist Nagy, and his stated approval of the armed Soviet intervention which crushed the Hungarian revolution (on November 4, 1956).

Kun's Communist reign, remembered with distaste amounting to repulsion by most of the population. As a result in 1945 the Communist ideology was sown on virgin soil in Hungary, with the more violent anti-Communist feelings being toned down by the nation's liberation through the Red Army, and pro-Communist tendencies kept in check by the unsavoury lesson of the past. Yet despite the diverse orientations of the various East European Satellites, their history under Soviet rule tended to mould their political thinking into a common pattern. Hence it could come about that the representative majority of the Hungarian people did not assume a significantly different attitude toward the Soviet Union in 1956 than did the populations of the other Satellites. In fact, there were no major factors to which a reason for the revolt could be ascribed operating in Hungary since 1945, which would not have been at work elsewhere. The standard of existence was not lower in Hungary than in most other Satellites – as a matter of fact, it was even lower in Bulgaria and Rumania. The national feelings of the Hungarians were not hurt either more or less by the ideological reverence for Russia and the presence of the Red Army on national soil, than the feelings of other countries: the ideological line was roughly the same everywhere, while there were Soviet troops also in Poland and Rumania. Hungary had known bloody purges, but they did not exceed those of elsewhere; the Slansky trial in Chechoslovakia and the Kostov trial in Bulgaria were a match for the Rajk process in Hungary. Rákosi, Gerö, Révai, Farkas and other Hungarian Party bosses were neither adhering more closely to the Kremlin line nor were more clumsy in carrying out its orders than Chervenkov in Bulgaria, Enver Hoxha in Albania, or Gheorghiu-Dey in Rumania. Hungary did have close ties with the West in its national tradition, but those of Chechoslovakia were even closer. Hungary is not a Slavic country, but neither is Rumania (a relatively docile Satellite), while Slavic Yugoslavia has unceremoniously broken with the Kremlin. The orientation of Hungary had been strongly anti-Communistic during the preceding Horthy-regime, but then the population of what is now East-Germany, was even more so prior to 1945. There are no major factors apparent with respect to Hungary which could have influenced the political thinking of the Hungarian people in a direction fundamentally different from the thinking of any other People's Democracy. Consequently the demands made by the Hungarian people in their brief spell of freedom should give an insight into the mode of thinking characterizing all East-European Satellites when due allowance for their historical and cultural peculiarities is made.

It is evident today that the revolt was not consciously prepared, but had an entirely spontaneous character. Basically, it was the Party system's explosion by gradually built-up pressures needing only minor and in themselves insignificant events to ignite. The demands were formulated in the heat of turbulent emotions by groups from all social strata, and broadcast without further refinement. Notwithstanding their divergent origins they manifest striking similarities. By proceeding through the elimination of purely local factors the field can be narrowed down to present a picture of the typical objectives of a collectivist people dominated by a foreign power.

The predominance of localized factors in a national revolt results to a large extent from a lack of organization among the insurgents, giving individuals with personal grievances or particular desires the chance to express themselves in the name of a more inclusive group.

When the group finds a representative spokesman, however, then under local factors the common features of all members of the group must be understood. And when the representative majority of all organized groups in a nation integrates its voice in the formulation of wishes and demands, then we may assume that the voice of the nation is heard.

The striking feature of the demands of the Hungarian revolution was national unity. From October 23, 1956, the first day of the revolution, the Hungarian people issued demands in an astonishing volume. At first these demands were circulated in the form of handbills, brief tracts, formulated as manifestos and resolutions. Later, the revolutionaries seized radio stations and demands were broadcast incessantly, almost every hour of the day. The radio broadcasts were monitored abroad without exception, and thus provide the best source of information. They are also the most reliable, since the radio stations were undoubtedly in the hands of those who had the broadest popular backing. The astonishing fact about the broadcasts is their virtual unanimity on major issues. While stations differed in political orientation (Radio Free Miskolc for example appears to have represented the Hungarian "left," while Radio Free Györ the "center" – or in comparison to the general tenor of the revolution, the "right"), they stood united on the major issues. The growth of cohesion among the revolutionary forces was rapid. Within a matter of days "revolutionary councils," "worker's councils," "Kolkhoz councils," and "student

parliaments" sprung up and began functioning as a counter-govern-
ment. At first these organizations were relatively isolated. It did not
take more than a few days, however, before they established contact
by courier and later by radio. The major body of the demands were
broadcast with the knowledge of all representative bodies of the
people, and the unanimity of the demands corresponded to the general
opinion of the people. The Special Committee of the United Nations
concluded that: "In the interval between 23 October and 4 November
1956, the voice of the Hungarian people was heard in organizations
which appeared or reappeared in the climate of freedom which spread
through the country in those ten days. Contrary to what might have
been expected, the voice that spoke through these organizations was
harmonious, rather than discordant. The Committee has no doubt
that this was the expression of the will of the Hungarian people and
that the organizations of workers, of farmers, of writers and of youth
were representative of the Hungarian people." [1]

There were altogether 225 instances of broadcast demands. They
centred on the following issues: [2]

Withdrawal of Soviet Troops National Independence	 78	35% of Total
Political Reform Organizational Reform Economic Reform Personal Demands Symbolic Demands	132	59%
Special Demands	 15	6%

(All percentages rounded.) We shall examine these demands one by
one.[3]

Demands for the Withdrawal of Soviet Troops from Hungary

All demands were contingent on the presence of Soviet troops on
Hungarian soil. All strata of the population realized that the success
of whatever demands they might make would depend on whether the
Red Army intervened or not. Hence the basic as well as instrumental

---

[1] *Report of the Special Committee on the Problem of Hungary*, General Assembly, Eleventh
Session, par. 708.

[2] Based on data furnished by The Hungarian Committee, New York, in *Facts about
Hungary*, I. Kovács, editor (1959).

[3] Based on the text and classification of *A Szabadságharc Követelései* (V. Juhász) Free
Europe Press (1956).

demand of the entire revolution was that of the withdrawal of Soviet troops. The demand was basic in that Soviet troops in Hungary were a prime factor of hurt national feelings, a major blot on the social consciousness of the country; it was instrumental in that no further demands could be submitted with reasonable chance of success until such a time as Soviet troops had withdrawn from national territory.

The first time this demand received recognition in a public message was on October 25 at 15.18 hours when Prime Minister Imre Nagy announced: "The withdrawal of Soviet forces whose intervention will shortly establish the Socialist order, will take place immediately after the reestablishment of order." (The ambiguity of the term "Socialist order" fully realized by the population, reflects the ambiguity of the entire Socialist system divided as it is between the ambitions of the people and the directives of the Party.) The second time this demand figured in the news was already on the following day: Nagy announced his acceptance of the demands of the people of the county of Borsod. In these demands the statementfigures: "We demand that Soviet units be withdrawn from Hungary until January 1 at the latest." This is already an unconditional demand, an ultimatum not assigning any beneficent role to Soviet troops. Later that day (October 26) Radio Kossuth (Budapest) repeatedly demanded the withdrawal of Soviet troops in conjunction with the establishment of the independent status of the country. On October 27 this demand took the first place in the broadcast of an unidentified rebel Radio. Radio Free Györ, being controlled at the time by the National Council of Györ, demanded the *immediate* withdrawal of Soviet troops. From the following day on, the demand was hourly repeated, and was taken over by Radio Kossuth as well. This day (October 29) was the witness of the first demand made for the dissolution of Hungary's obligations incurred under the Warsaw Pact. (The Warsaw Pact served as valid excuse for stationing Russian troops in Hungary. These troops were to defend the interest of the Warsaw Pact nations in the event of a "counterrevolutionary" uprising.)

Henceforth practically all broadcasts listed the withdrawal of Soviet troops as the first point of their demands, although less radical groups asked for the restoration of order in the interest of the immediate beginning of talks between the Hungarian and Soviet governments to effect the withdrawal. It is significant that these troops were denoted as "foreign" by the ultimatum of the miners of Lovász, emphasizing that Soviet forces represented intervention by a *foreign* power in

Hungary's internal affairs. Other demands asked for the "full and final" removal of the troops, and required that the Soviet government announce this to "world opinion." Imre Nagy's message of October 28 included the statement that his government had reached agreement with that of the Soviet Union as to the withdrawal of Soviet troops from Budapest, and was about to undertake talks concerning their withdrawal from national territory.

The Intellectual's Revolutionary Committee neatly summed up national feelings in a broadcast of Kossuth Radio on October 29: "Hungarians! There might be difference of opinion between us, but we agree on the most important demand: we demand the following: the government should adjust our relations with the Soviet Union on the basis of equal rights. Soviet troops should begin withdrawing from the entire territory of the nation." The former Party-organ Szabad Nép formulated the same sentiment in more ardent terms in a leading article of the same day: "...why could it not be realized earlier that the whole folk wants with ardent, during many years suppressed, but now irrepressible passion, that Soviet troops should be withdrawn from our country's territory."

On October 30 Radio Györ invoked armed might in its demand: "... (if Soviet troops are not withdrawn) the air force of the People's army will support the Hungarian worker's demands with its arms." On the same day the menace of a general strike was made to lend weight to this demand by the workers of the town of Szombathely (broadcast by Radio Györ). On October 31 Imre Nagy appealed to the Hungarian people to abstain from manifesting provocation, disturbance and animosity, in order to aid the retreat of Soviet troops from Hungary. (A provincial Radio added zealously that the population should prepare signposts in all communities to point the way to the shortest road to Russia ...) At the height of fighting the demand for the withdrawal of Soviet troops was becoming frantic – it was becoming increasingly evident that Soviet troops were not only still present, but more were coming in. On November 3 Cardinal Mindszenty appealed to the Soviet leaders' common sense in asking them to consider that the Hungarian people would esteem the Soviet folk higher if they were not crushed by their troops. However, the revolution was quashed and János Kádár's puppet regime attempted to win popular support by including the above demand in its programme. In these "false demands" the withdrawal of the troops was always subjected to the restoration of law and order: today we shall obey,

and tomorrow we shall talk of independence. Yet it was only too pain-
fully clear that Hungary would have no more trumps to play against
the Kremlin if the people returned to their work under Soviet control.

Demands of National Independence

This category of demands forms a basic component of the objectives
of the Hungarian people during the revolution. It was less frequently
uttered than the demand for the withdrawal of Soviet troops, for it
could have a chance of being respected only if the other demand met
with success. Demands of national independence were perhaps the
most fundamental of all the demands expressed in printed or broadcast
messages and circulated as hand-tracts during these turbulent days.
Fulfillment of this demand was a precondition to all further objectives,
just as the withdrawal of Soviet troops was a precondition for the
independence of Hungary.

Hungary's national independence, the demands emphasized, was
to rest on equal and friendly relations with all countries, including the
Soviet Union, the East European People's Republics, Western Europe,
and the United States. (If equal relations with Yugoslavia were particularly emphasized this was due to the fear of a dominant Yugoslav
influence in Hungary's internal affairs following a recent Hungarian-
Yugoslav agreement.)

On October 26 the Central Committee of the Hungarian Workers'
(Communist) Party announced: "The new government shall begin
negotiations with the Soviet government on the basis of independence,
complete equality, and non-interference in internal affairs to settle
relations between our countries." The demand for equality with the
Soviet Union was heard several times over the air on this and on the
following day. On October 28 Radio Kossuth joined the demand for
independence to the demand for the withdrawal of Soviet troops. Radio
Free Győr declared: "The government of our country should agree
with the government of the Soviet Union that henceforth we shall act in
all questions by respecting the mutual sovereignty of the two countries
and the principle of non-interference in each other's internal affairs."

The same day Imre Nagy's speech was broadcast by Radio Kossuth.
The Premier said among other things: "The Hungarian government
has started negotiations to settle relations between the Hungarian
People's Republic and the Soviet Union with regard to the withdrawal
of Soviet forces stationed in Hungary. All this is in the spirit of Soviet-

Hungarian friendship and the principle of mutual equality and national independence of Socialist countries."

The following day several requests were made to re-examine all contacts on the basis of mutual equality. On October 30 a more radical demand was made for the first time: the Radio of the county of Borsod requested that the United Nations should examine Soviet interference in the affairs of Hungary. At the same time Radio Kossuth threatened that armed force would be employed against all internal or foreign enemies menacing the nation's independence. News spread at this time that Soviet troops had not left Hungarian soil, but were actually preparing for a new attack. A communiqué of the Borsod workers' council and student parliament broadcast by Radio Miskolc stated: "In the present situation the Soviet Union severely violates the Warsaw Pact and the UN Charter... The Hungarian people ask the UN to intervene immediately in the interest of Hungary." Radio Kossuth broadcast the request on the following day that "Our country must be neutral, like Austria and Switzerland." The provincial Radios echoed: "Hungary is a neutral state." Various schools, organizations and newly formed political bodies insisted on this point as well. During the days that followed a status like that of Switzerland and Austria was repeatedly demanded for Hungary, and the UN was asked to take note of this, and to send economic and, if necessary, military aid to insure it.

The tract of the Revolutionary Youth Party released on November 2 demands as its first item: "The full independence and neutrality of our country." On November 3 Cardinal Mindszenty's broadcast expressed gratitude for the sympathy of the other nations of the world, and stated: "... we, a small nation wish to exist in friendship, in undisturbed, mutual esteem with the great United States of America, as well as with the powerful Russian Empire. In good neighbourly relations with Prague, Bucharest, Warsaw and Belgrade."

On November 3 the revolutionary council of the Hungarian Foreign Ministry proposed to the Premier measures to insure the *perpetual neutrality* of Hungary. When it was evident that the revolution's cause was lost, Imre Nagy summarized the demands of Hungary's independence for the West in 3 points (November 4): *Hungary repudiates the Warsaw Pact; Hungary declares itself a neutral state; Hungary places itself under the protection of the UN.*

Demands of Political Reform

Demands of political reform presuppose the success of the revolution insofar as Hungary's autonomy is concerned. These demands give a first indication of the kind of social structure the Hungarian people wanted in 1956. The formulation of the demands centred on 2 major issues: free, secret elections; and the admission of the voice of the people into the government's political programme. Both formulations were directed against the Communist totalitarian system. Whether they were also directed against the social principles explicated by Communist theory we shall see presently, – that much is certain that the two must never be confused.

On October 23 and 25 the general demand for "The Hungarian Way to Socialism" was heard several times. It should be noted in this context that "Socialism" is equated in official ideological terminology with the present stage of Communism, hence the word has a double meaning, one of which refers to the Kremlin-directed Communist system, and the other to a mode of social organization. Very likely for this reason more than anything else, the word "Socialism" was relatively seldom heard during the Revolution.

Imre Nagy announced in a broadcast over Radio Kossuth on October 25: "Soon after the restoration of order the National Assembly will be called. At that session I will submit an all-embracing and basic programme of reform. This programme will embrace all important problems of our national life. This programme demands the reorganization of the government on the basis of the unification of broad democratic national forces represented by the reorganized Patriotic People's Front." Nagy evidently wished to express by this rather obscure formulation his intention to effect the transition to a multi-party system. It must be remembered that the one-party system is a typical characteristic of every totalitarian regime.

On October 26 Radio Kossuth still insisted on "the Hungarian Way to Socialism." The same idea cropped up in a different formulation as the demand for a "Socialist Democracy." On this day was the demand for the election of free workers' councils in factories expressed for the first time. On October 27 all revolutionary Radio stations demanded free elections. Radio Kossuth asked for free elections to take place subsequent to the withdrawal of Soviet troops (October 28). Radio Free Miskolc demanded the reestablishment of all political parties which belonged to the National Front in 1945, and free elections on the basis of the free functioning of all parties. The Radio of the county of Borsod expressed the wish for an "independent, autonomous government," without participation of the members of the previous Rákosi regime. The miners of Transdanubia stated that they had no objection to Communists participating on the list of free elections: the people would decide in which party to place their confidence.

The worker's council of Borsod county summarized the people's demands: "We demand the formation of a government that fights for a truly democratic, independent, autonomous, free and socialist Hungary, without the presence of the Ministers of the Rákosi regime." The council also demanded the reduction of the State apparatus: "In the present situation there is no need for 22 Ministries and 3 Deputy Ministers..." It is significant that the oversized cabinet was known to serve totalitarian politics, and its reduction was thus held to contribute to a more democratic State organization. Radio Kossuth commented Nagy's announcement on October 28 thus: "Only the government of an independent country can build Socialism corresponding to Hungary's specific features." On the following day Radio Free Miskolc demanded the reduction of the size of the cabinet, and inclusion of the people's demands in the government's programme. The students of Sopron University announced that they wanted a "Free, independent, democratic Hungary, wherein all power really belongs to the working people." Similar demands were broadcast by all revolutionary Radios. Radio Free Szombathely asked that "The government should start talks with persons from the ranks of the freedom fighters, the present combination of persons in the government must cease." Free elections and the admission of the people's demands into the government's programme were insistently demanded on the following days. On October 31 a new note was struck by Radio Kossuth in that it demanded free elections "without foreign control." Various councils and revolutionary organizations took up this demand in which the predicate "foreign" could only have applied to the Soviet Union.

The workers' council of the counties of Szabolcs-Szatmár sent a message to the free people of the world in which they named as their goal their old party-programme, which included human rights, free speech, respect of religious creeds, free press and the right to hold meetings and to strike. Similar programmes were envisaged by various demands broadcast until the end of the brief spell of freedom. On November 3 Cardinal Mindszenty's speech contained the following relevant passage: "The fight for freedom has taken place because the nation wanted to decide freely its way of life, its destiny, the governing of its State, the realization of the fruits of its labour . . . this country needs many things, but not many parties and party-leaders . . . we live in a constitutional state, in a classless society, we are developing democratic conditions, we support private ownership which is rightly and justly limited by social interests . . . we want to be a nation with an exclusively cultural-national spirit."

Demands of Organizational Reform

Demands of this type dealt with specific aspects of Party and State organization, and while they had a smaller scope than demands for national independence, they give us a more accurate insight into the political thinking of the people. While it may be held that national independence, the removal of foreign troops and autonomous government in the best interest of the people are fundamental desires of all nations, there can be no doubt that the type of organizations a people hold to be best suited to realize these wishes delimit particular modes of political thought, and give a clue as to the political orientation of the nation.

Basic of all demands in this category was the insistence on the workers' autonomy in the factories. (This demand could have had far reaching consequences, most likely leading to the reorganization of the social structure on the Yugoslav pattern. The Soviet-controlled Party-system has been against admitting any interference in administrative matters in the factories, as in the affairs of the Party, by workers' organizations.) At the opening phase of the revolution on October 23, Radio Kossuth (then known as Radio Liberty) listed among its demands: "The autonomy of the workers in factories and workshops." Success of this demand was in a large measure determined by the elimination of the Party's power, incorporated by the security police (AVH), hated on this account, as well as for its ruthless practices. Radio Free Miskolc formulated the demand on October 25: "We demand the reorganization of the security forces . . . We have had enough of the autocracy of certain leaders." The following day Radio Györ repeated: "The security forces must be disbanded. The army and police should guarantee order."

The first demand dealing with the newly established workers' councils was heard on October 26: "Every factory and workshop should freely elect workers' councils". At the same time the demand for the immediate dissolution of the AVH was often repeated. Premier Nagy could announce on October 28: "The government supports

those new organs of democratic self-government which the people
have started and will strive to find a place for them in the administrative machinery ... New armed forces will be formed from units of
the Army, of the police, and of the armed workers' and youth groups."
Radio Kossuth reported later that day that "The Hungarian National
Committee has been formed today. Its task is to unite and coordinate
the work of locally elected revolutionary councils and of the autonomous national committees." The Revolutionary Committee of the
Intellectuals demanded: "The trade unions must become organizations
that really represent the workers' interests, and have a freely elected
organization."

Radio Free Szombathely broadcast the following day: We call on
the workers ... to voice their demands in disciplined meetings in their
work places ... We, the National Committee of the County Vas ...
declare that we want a free, independent, Democratic and Socialist
Hungary headed by the government of Imre Nagy."

On October 31 Radio Kossuth transmitted the message of the
Hungarian Committee concerning the steps taken to work out a new
Constitution. The Radio of the county of Borsod asked that henceforth "the local councils should set up the local security forces." On
November 1 Radio Kossuth repeated this demand, adding that the
members of the AVH must be excluded from the new police force. The
Radio also broadcast the information that in the interest of the trade-
unions' reorganization former social-democratic union leaders were
conducting the talks.

Demands of Economic Reform

Demands of economic reform are numerically the most important
of the various categories of demands expressed during the revolution.
They give relatively little information as to the political thinking of
the people, however, since most of these demands were due to the low
standard of living in Hungary, and proposed reforms which could
improve the economic situation of the country.

It is evident from these demands that the people entertained no
illusions as to why their standard of living was so low: the exploitation
of Hungary's economy by the Soviet Union was generally known and
blamed. The direct object of accusations was the Hungarian Workers'
(Communist) Party: the leaders of the Party had tolerated this shame-
less exploitation. Demands of economic reform are significant for this
analysis insofar as they foresaw specific measures to remedy the actual
situation. While these measures were to a large extent dictated by

good economic sense (as the realization of the yield of Hungarian uranium mines by Hungarians, free trade at realistic prices with other countries, etc.), the immediate means of putting the reforms into effect indicate the type of thinking current among the people. We shall only quote here the series of demands made during October 28 which was to a large extent typical of all demands of economic relevance made during the ten-day period. "The uranium mines and other national treasures (bauxite) must be placed at the service of the country." "The reform of agriculture." "Workers' autonomy in the factories as well as in the trade unions." "The cessation of the compulsory surrender of agricultural produce." "Higher pay, higher standard of living." "The development of housing." "Higher pensions and family bonus." "The reduction of taxes and the elimination of taxes for childlessness." "Collectivization on a free-will basis." "The elimination of (prescribed) quotas." "Better working conditions for women."

Personal Demands

Personal demands dealt with the liberation of political prisoners, the return of deportees from the Soviet Union, and with members of the government. We shall list here only those demands that dealt with public figures, and aimed at the better future of the country through entrusting the reins of power to reliable and trustworthy leaders. These demands were either negative or positive. Negative demands asked for the removal of unpopular leaders (mostly those of the former Rákosi regime), while positive demands asked for particular politicians. These demands took many forms, but had a remarkable homogeneous content: Negative demands centred on the removal of "Rákosists" and positive demands concentrated on the reinstatement of Imre Nagy as Premier. A correct evaluation of these demands can only be made if the relevance of Rákosi and Nagy to the Hungarian people is clear to us. Now Rákosi was generally known as the Hungarian Stalin; he was fond of referring to himself as Stalin's favourite pupil. The blame that the people put on the Party for their troubles centred largely on the person of Rákosi. In addition to his other deeds, he was also responsible for killing Imre Nagy's popular New Course Program with the March and April 1955 Resolutions: these marked Rákosi's return to power. The Rákosi-Nagy fight dated at least from July 4, 1953 (when Nagy had become Premier) and was well known to all. Thus siding with Nagy also meant the condemnation of Rákosi, and all that the latter stood for. But what was so attractive in Nagy's own ideas that he had almost the entire population unanimously behind him? His views are contained in a 115.000 word dissertation addressed to his former Comrades on the Central Committee, written by him during his forced retirement before the Revolution. It contains Nagy's beliefs with respect to the Party, Stalinism, his own New Course, and the needs of the Hungarian people. The work indicates that Imre Nagy, despite all his anger and his accusation of Stalinism, Rákosi, and Party politics, remained a dedicated, firmly convinced Communist (when the word is taken to apply to the theory, rather than to the actual practice of world-Communism). His thesis is filled with quotations from the "Classics" of his day: Marx, Lenin and Stalin. He considered his New Course to have incorporated the very essence of good Marxism-Leninism, and that Marxism-Leninism alone could point the way to a better future for the Hungarian people. The text has been examined by reliable experts in the West, and is found to be unquestionably authentic. We quote here merely those passages which characterize his views with respect to the position from which we examine the Revolution, and which we hold to have been its major causal factor.[1]

"We Hungarian Communists will faithfully cultivate and forever endorse the historical Marxist Communist motto "Workers of the world unite!" but to it we shall add the motto expressed in the "Szózat" (written in 1836 by the patriot Mihály Vörösmarty) reflecting deep national feeling and love of country: "Hungarians, remain unflinchingly faithful to your fatherland"."

"A People's Democracy is a democratic type of dictatorship of the proletariat. If methods used by the Soviets under entirely different circumstances are copied in imitation in a People's Democracy – and this has taken place in all the People's Democracies but particularly so in Hungary–then the People's Democracy ceases to have the nature of a proletarian dictatorship. Such a country also thus loses the characteristics required by the situation as it actually exists in that particular nation. To a great extent this happened in the people's democratic countries and it has given rise to serious obstacles in the stabilization of construction."

"The leaders of the Party and the country must understand that the fate of the nation and the fate of the people is identical. The people cannot be free if the nation is not independent, if it does not possess complete sovereignty, if foreign influences prevail in its internal

---

[1] Imre Nagy, *On Communism*, London, 1957. Our quotations follow the clearer wording of the translation in *East Europe*, Vol. 6, No. 7.

affairs; and no nation can be independent and sovereign if its people do not completely possess the right to freedom."

"The violent contrast between words and deeds, between principles and their realization, is rocking the foundations of our People's Democracy, our society, and our Party. This contrast, of which the people are becoming ever more conscious, is leading to dissension and loss of faith among the masses, who hope for a better, happier and more peaceful life, for the realization of the truly high ideals of Socialism. The working people are unable to reconcile the rapid progress of Socialism with the deterioration, or at least the stagnation, of their standard of living."

Many more quotations could be added. These should suffice to show, however, the reason for at least one aspect of Nagy's popularity. The demands expressed for Imre Nagy during the Revolution were demands for the realization of such ideas.

Symbolic Demands

Symbolic demands did not request actual reforms or changes, but served to express the people's sentiment with respect to specific symbolic objects and events. Such demands hardly varied throughout the Revolution (nor for a long time thereafter). They can be treated under two collective headings as follows: (i) Demands to remove the hammer and sickle from the Hungarian flag and adopt the so-called Kossuths arms (used in the 1848–49 revolution when Hungary fought against the Austrian monarchy). (ii) Demands to have March 15 (the proclamation of the 1848 Revolution), October 6 (the day 13 Hungarian high officers of that revolution were executed owing to Tsarist interference in the Austro-Hungarian fight), and October 23 (the first day of the present Revolution) proclaimed National Holidays.

While with the demands for National Holidays no spontaneous action could be taken, the intensity with which these objectives were demanded was fully evidenced by all people in cutting out the Soviet emblem from all flags, uniforms, decorations, and from wherever it was found.

Special Demands

These demands dealt with some specific problem and had relatively little to do with large-scale reforms. Herein figure the demands of the border guards to wear Hungarian uniforms, the Army's demand to change the stripes of officers (those actually used resembled the Red

Army's stripes), and demands for religious freedom. The greater part
of such isolated demands were taken up by university students'
demands for pedagogic reforms. These centred on the abolishment
of compulsory subjects directly associated with the totalitarian methods of the Party: the compulsory teaching of Marxism-Leninism,
of the Russian language, obligatory physical education programmes
and the like. Students also demanded better food and better school
buildings, new textbooks (particularly new history books, as those
written under the "cult of personality" were obnoxious) and freedom
to express their views and to choose their subjects of study.

Evaluation

The above were by no means all the demands made by the Hungarian
people during their ten days of freedom between October 23 and
November 4, 1956. These are, however, representative of the kinds
of demands made, and the political objectives of the Hungarian people
may be assessed from them. We can subdivide the demands into two
general categories: the demands expressing dissatisfaction with a
particular fact, event, state of affairs, arrangement or person; and the
demands manifesting a desire to see certain facts, events, conditions,
and persons in given places and in specific roles. All demands to
remove, destroy, annull, abolish or dissolve have naturally a reverse,
constructive side, just as the demands to do, organize, assume functions,
adopt and establish have a destructive side: before the construction
of the new could begin the old has to be dismantled and disposed of.
Yet not all destructive demands found their counterparts in constructive ones, nor was this the case *vice versa*. Although the reverse side
of each demand may be surmised, let us proceed on the basis of facts,
and evaluate the demands as they were made. Hence we shall have
two general categories: the "negative" and the "positive" demands.
Under the heading of negative demands we shall subsume the demands
to withdraw Soviet troops from national territory, dissolve the
Warsaw Pact, remove Soviet influence, equalize relations with the
Soviet Union and with all other countries of the Socialist bloc and the
West as well. We shall subsume the demands of "National Independence" under the negative category since independence is essentially the absence of external determination. A state does not have to be
organized in a particular way to be independent, nor do its internal
affairs have any direct bearing on its international status: a state is
independent when there are no outside forces exerting an undue and

purposive influence on its internal development. Hungary was not independent prior to the Revolution, and the reason for this was Soviet foreign policy, although the fault that this policy could be put into practice may (or may not) have been with Hungary's internal structure and the leaders in whose hands the decisions lay. National independence for Hungary meant the negatian of Soviet influence, rather than the construction of any order or system within the country. Insofar as internal construction was concerned, its role was to negotiate the removal and guarantee the continued absence of foreign interference. Hence the withdrawal of Soviet troops as the precondition, and equalized relations with the Soviet Union as the realization, of Hungary's independence was a negative demand: it aimed at eliminating existing and unsatisfactory conditions.

Further negative demands were made to oust the Rákosi regime and his Party-*apparatchiki*. There was little doubt in the people's minds that Rákosi and his associates were installed and kept in power by Stalin, by Soviet pressure exerted through the Red Army. Removal of these people was essentially equal to the removal of Soviet troops: both represented unwelcome foreign influence in the nation's internal affairs. The same applies to all demands to abolish organizations, remove practices and discard symbols developed and installed either by the Party directly, or through the influence of the Party. The hated security police AVH was a Party-backed organization, such practices as compulsory Russian and Marxism-Leninism instruction in schools and the hammer and sickle as well as the red star on the national arms of Hungary were all due to Party orders.

Under the positive heading we can subsume the demands outlining political reform, organizational reform, economic reform, calling specific personages to leading positions, and making propositions to organize councils, distribute influence, hold elections, reinstate reasonable economic practices, create a constitution, have State and UN representation corresponding to the people's interests and acting as their mouthpiece, liberal schooling, unbiased text-books, national style uniforms, and many more.

On checking through these categories the striking conclusion emerges that demands under both headings are, in great lines, almost entirely homogeneous. If we subtract demands which have general human reasons behind them (such as better economic policies, no cruelty, no deportations and the like), we shall find that what we have termed "negative" demands are all motivated by a distinct and unmistakable patriotism, amounting at times to a veritable passion, but never sinking below the level of prime motivation. What the Hungarian people did *not* want was foreign interference and exploitation: that emerges as the most fundamental negative objective of the revolutionaries. Not only the demands formulated by the people, but the views of the leader the people demanded, confirm this: whatever else he may have been, Nagy was definitely a patriot. That much is safe to assume, that the primary motivation of all negative demands was national sentiment first, and only secondly economic or intellectual penury and whatever dissatisfactions there existed besides. (Would the prime motivation have been the low standard of living, for example, the revolutionaries would have negotiated with the representatives of the Hungarian and Soviet governments for better terms under the Warsaw Pact, and would at least have tried to improve the existing situation. Similar moves would have been likely if we assume that the prime motivation was anything other than nationalist feeling.)

The positive demands are no less homogeneous when we take the type of political scheme of which they give evidence. Deducting again all universally human demands (better housing, less taxes, higher standard of existence, free press, freedom to choose the subjects of study, etc.) the manner in which the State, the political parties, the trade-unions, the factories, the agriculture and most cultural fields were to be run was decidedly Marxist, though nationalist: it resembled the Yugoslav pattern more than any other. Most of the positive demands appear to have been formulated by the writers and students: the revolutionary elite of the intelligentsia. As the UN Report on Hungary states: "The students thus became, with the writers, a mouthpiece for the Hungarian people as a whole. Their objective was not to criticize the principles of Communism as such. Rather, as Marxists, they were anxious to show that the system of government obtaining in Hungary was a perversion of what they held to be true Marxism ... The influence of the students immediately before the uprising helped to give it an emphasis on youth which was to remain characteristic of it. When the phase of protest meetings and street demonstrations changed into that of actual fighting, it was still the younger generation, this time the young workers, who played the most prominent part. Most of the witnesses questioned by the Committee were under 35 years of age and many of them were considerably younger. It was this same age group, which had been indoctrinated along Party lines, whose enthusiasm made and sustained the Hungarian uprising." [1]

Not only the "mouthpieces" of the uprising, but also the widest social strata gave evidence of the type of thinking characteristic of Marxism (i.e. of collectivism) in that most people built and supported the revolutionary workers' councils, national committees, local committees, student parliaments, and the many local organizations going under innumerable names. "Regarding the attitude taken by the Councils toward the (Communist) Party [reports the UN Special Committee] the following comments of Hétföi Hirlap of 29 October are significant: "The demands (of the Revolutionary Councils) are, on the whole, identical and essentially *socialist and democratic* in their character, and do not intend to destroy the people's power. This is proved by the fact that wherever Party organizations endorsed the aims of the democratic revolution, no action was taken against them." [2] Radio Györ stated a generally acknowledged view when it said on October 28: "This is not a counterrevolution, but the national movement of the Hungarian people. The workers and peasants in Györ-Sopron counties do not want the restoration of the power of manufacturers and landlords; the national revolution is not aimed at the restoration of the old regime." The prime motivation of positive demands appears to be the creation of a Socialist state in the spirit of Marxist collectivism. Since nationalism emerges as the prime motivation of negative demands (35% of the total made during the Revolution), and collectivism as the major impetus of positive constructive demands (59% of total), the objectives of the Hungarian revolutionaries, and of the whole people represented by the revolutionary avant-garde, may be termed *national collectivist*.

This assertion may appear surprising in view of the conclusion usually drawn as to the objectives of the Hungarian Revolution. A certain and quite unnecessary confusion arises from an unanalysed use of the word "freedom." The Hungarian Revolution was undoubtedly a "Szabadságharc," a fight for freedom. This was not the first fight for freedom the Hungarian people undertook; their history is replete with such spontaneous and heroic upsurges, the last major one taking place in 1848. When we consider the 1956 uprising exclusively as a fight for freedom, we shall see only the aspect of the revolt which aimed at breaking the country's captivity, and which was thus entirely

[1] *Op. cit.*, par. 397–8.
[2] *Ibid.*, par. 501 (italics in original).

anti-Soviet. Since the Western democracies are also anti-Soviet in sentiment, the equation came quite naturally: the Hungarians are anti-Soviet, *therefore* they share the West's conception of existence. The proof of this equation was the insistent use of the word "freedom" by the revolutionaries.

The 1956 Revolution was undoubtedly a fight for freedom, but it was also something else. Every captive society, just as all captive persons, desire freedom. They express a demand which has for its objective the *negation* of the chains of captivity. If and when that negation is effected, just what the societies do with their freedom is still as open to question as what a person leaving prison will do. The demands of the Revolution which we have subsumed under the negative heading and termed the "nationalist" demands, represent the aspect of the Revolution as a fight for freedom. This is the aspect of the uprising which was directed *against* something – there is, however, also an aspect which was directed *for* something. The uprising was termed a fight for freedom by the revolutionaries themselves, and this fact has been much publicized in the Western world. Yet these same revolutionaries have called their movement a "revolution" as much, if not more, than a fight for freedom, and added to the word "revolution" the adjectives "socialist," "democratic," "socialist-democratic."

It was also emphasized that this was *not* a counterrevolution. Not "counter" to what? one may ask. It was certainly counter to the Soviet policy of directing Hungary's internal affairs. It was also counter to the leaders of the Party in Hungary. It was *not* counter to the collectivist principles of Communism, however. The revolutionaries wished to apply these principles correctly, to make them serve the nation's, and not the Soviet bloc's interests. The main reason why this fact did not emerge with greater clarity may have been a simple one, yet it could be the reason why such revolutions do not break out more often, and when they do break out, do not succeed fully. This reason is that ideologically indoctrinated and at the same time oppressed people have no concepts at their disposal to express their strivings and consolidate them in planned action. Communism has shown what power a system of concepts represents in world politics. Communist ideology has annexed the greatest possible number of general concepts to suit its purpose: Democracy, Socialism, Communism, Dictatorship, Republic, Proletariat, Peasantry, and many more are, in the Communist interpretation, so many components of mankind's inevitable march toward Communism. The generally used concepts not included in the positive use of the ideology –Bourgeoisie, Capitalism, Imperialism, Colonialism, Autocracy, Class-society, etc. take on an all-black character, contrasting with the pure white of pro-Communist concepts. The fact is that Communist ideology uses almost all concepts capable of political application either as pro-Communist and pro-Soviet, or anti-Communist and anti-Soviet. Now when people accept the collectivist principles of Communism without accepting the Kremlin's totalitarian application thereof, they find themselves without concepts to express their ideas. They do not wish to use pro-Communist concepts, for these are intimately associated with Soviet and Party-interests – and these people are anti-Soviet and also anti-Party in the measure that their Party is pro-Soviet. Consequently the concepts of Socialism, Socialist-Democracy, Dictatorship and Proletariat, are all tinged with an unwished for sideflavour. On the other hand the concepts of Bourgeois Democracy, Democracy plain, or Democracy and Republic as exemplified by Western states are also unsuitable: they are contrary to the people's accepted idea of society. (That Hungary asked for a status like that of Austria and Switzerland is not to be taken as meaning to imitate their social structure: this was merely an expedient measure to clarify that Hungary wished to be independent of all foreign influence.) The Hungarian Revolution was known by several names, of which only two: Szabadságharc and Felkelés (Fight for Freedom and Uprising) were used consequently and with full conviction. Just what kind of an uprising it was could be stated unanimously only by putting it negatively: it was *not* a counterrevolution. A meeting of the MEFESZ'[1] "temporary committee" of the Technological University after the Revolution gave evidence of these difficulties very clearly.[2] Under discussion at the meeting was the MEFESZ programme – a proposition which aside from the here quoted article never reached the public. One part of the programme stated: "We fight for Socialism, we want the Socialist system of organization." Someone objected, "the words "we fight for Socialism" must be scratched out, for they repeat the idea expressed in the subsequent words." The motion was accepted. "But who speaks in the name of Socialism?" Someone suggested: "There are some who say Socialism, but without Communists. We must avoid this." The issue is voted on: the proposition is found

[1] Federation of Hungarian University Students.
[2] Reported in *Népszabadsàg*, Budapest, January 4, 1957.

pointless, it is a mere play with words." The question whether *any* counterrevolution took place in Hungary was then debated [the government of János Kádár claimed at this time that the entire movement was motivated by counterrevolutionaries] when the president of the Committee [formerly a fanatic Communist, Party member, now sincere revolutionary] remarked: "There are obstacles in the way of a clear definition. It is very difficult to express what we want. Let us leave the evaluation entirely. The old evaluation remains. If we do not speak of anything, then at least we do not slip backwards." As a result all definition of the Revolution was scratched out from the MEFESZ programme . . .

The Communist bloc was unanimous in defining the Revolution as a counterrevolution; the West understood it primarily as a fight for freedom. The tragedy of the Hungarian people, as the tragedy of all Soviet dominated and Communist-indoctrinated small nations, is that they cannot give expression to their ideas without being misunderstood. As soon as they claim to be Socialist, Marxist, or Social Democrats, the West considers them a potential threat to liberalism. And if they express anti-Soviet sentiments, the Soviet Union takes measures to eliminate the "revisionists" and "bourgeois counterrevolutionary infiltrators" from the national scene. Alone, without being able to define their principles in terms which could make it universally understandable, they fight a losing fight. This is certainly true of Hungary. The splendid and spontaneous national unity that found expression in the Revolutionary Workers' Councils was broken again: Kádár's puppet regime issued a law on November 21 (1956) which stripped the councils of all political power. They had been promised an economic role as organs of "worker self-management," but were not permitted to take over functions performed by factory directors or Party-controlled trade-union committees. The following day the workers called a 48-hour strike in reaction to the law, but to no avail. More strikes broke out and general unrest swept over the country. On December 9 the regime outlawed the Budapest Workers' Council as well as all councils outside factories, and declared martial law. On December 12 a general strike went into effect. But by this time the revolutionary movement was thoroughly broken by Soviet tanks, and the country slowly subsided into its former status of Soviet Satellite. The Soviet-sponsored Hungarian Workers' Party took over control of the situation. At first only the most incorrigible Stalinists, AVH members, police and army-officers joined and supported the

Party. Before the Revolution the Party had 900.000 members. According to official sources membership was at 100.000 in the beginning of 1957, but increased gradually to 400.000 by 1959. Political power was again in the hands of the old Party leadership, the same people who ruled under Stalin's "favourite son," Mátyás Rákosi. Kádár led the struggle against dogmatism and revisionism, the famous "fight on two fronts" announced by Krushchev. Despite – or rather because – of this tactic the country went steadily downhill in moral and economic standard, with the result that the regime was finally induced to introduce the liberalized program of "new politics" aimed at eliminating the worst of the Stalinist views and methods, and winning more adherents for the Party. Kádár instituted a highly intensifed training programme for the Party cadres, designed to reeducate old Stalinist *apparatchiki* for functions in the revised order. The relative failure of the training programme as a whole was shown by the 1961 elections, when 15–20% of the Party cadres were changed. Much of the old guard was gone (to the regret of Kádár, who is held to have entertained friendly feelings toward his former comrades) and some new blood entered the Party. The rank and file was still composed of handpicked trustworthy personages, however, selected by Kádár for their alliegance to the Moscow line.

The 8th Party Congress held in Budapest in November, 1962, gave a similar picture. Again, 20% of the Party leadership was dropped, but at the same time the number of leading functionaries was increased by 23% (from 120 to 148). Dropped were mostly those functionaries who could be accused of "dogmatism," i.e. those who still persisted in the old ways, and failed to come along with Kádár in his new politics. Aside from two new committees (one for state economy and the other for agitprop) little change in the Party organization and programme has been announced. It appears that Kádár could consolidate his position still further by improving the balance of power within the opposing factions of the Party. The regime will thus be able, in the immediate future at least, to carry out its political line. Just what kind of line the government follows is evident from Kádár's concluding speech at the 8th Congress. The Hungarian Workers' Party, said Kádár, identifies itself fully with Krushchev's politics. Concerning the dispute with China, Kádár affirmed that the Chinese Communists do not have the right to exaggerate their own importance, and place it in the forefront of the international Socialist movement. The first place in that movement belongs to the Communist Party of the Soviet Union, for that Party earned its right and role as leader in history. In holding the relations of each Communist Party to the CPSU the criterion of true proletarian internationalism, Kádár appealed to all Parties to dissociate themselves from the attitude of Peking, and strengthen their ties with Moscow.

Thus in just over six years' time, the Hungarian Workers' (Communist) Party has managed to secure the reins of political power in the country, and steers openly the Moscow course, condemning all endeavours arising out of the attitudes that fueled the 1956 Revolution as "revisionist fallacy"[1]. At the same time, however, dogmatism is also fought, and in some respects at least, the political climate has become more liberal of late. It is futile to try to estimate just how much effect on these developments the Revolution may have had, and whether or not the situation would be the same had it not taken place. If we admit the premiss that in all spontaneous popular movements the political thought of the people plays a major role, then all revolts and similar manifestations may be regarded as symptomatic of, and organically bound up with, the specific conditions influencing the evolution of political thought in each country. In that sense revolutions are neither won nor lost, for they remain basic expressions of integral societal processes, in the determination of which they play the major role, if not through an immediate *coup*, then in the long run. The motive forces of the Hungarian revolution are no less present today than they were in the Autumn of 1956, merely their ostensive effect is less discernible in day to day developments.

Summary

In this analysis we evaluate the objectives of the Hungarian revolt of 1956 as the spontaneous and wide spread expression of national collectivist thinking. *National* because the people fought for their national autonomy and independence, for freedom as a nation; and *collectivist* because they foresaw the utilization of their collective freedom in building a Socialist state. While abhorring foreign domination and exploitation, they wished to subordinate individual freedom to collective freedom, the liberty of the person to the good of the nation as a whole. The idea of the evil of uncontrolled ownership of private property (particularly of the forces of production and of land) has penetrated deeply into the social consciousness; the view

---

[1] Some 80.000 strategically located Soviet troops guard Hungary against such "fallacies" at present.

according to which history is made by the struggle of the propertyless workers with the exploiting classes has been generally accepted, and the prime positive development of our times was seen in the Socialist movement. Clear evidence of the people's collectivist mode of thinking was given not only by their views, but also by their action: the formation of Revolutionary Workers' Councils and the call for a convinced Marxist to head the government are the major signs of Hungary's wide-spread collectivist atmosphere.

The refusal of the one-party system for Hungary contradicts this assessment. However, the contradiction is only apparent. There was a very good reason for advocating the multi-party system in the minds of the people: not a leaning toward individualism as such, but an intrinsic fear of the evils that the one-party system can give rise to. A great many of the rebels, backed by the majority of thep opulation, wanted to make absolutely certain that definite guarantees would be at hand to prevent the return of a Rákosi-type dictatorship. A one-party system, when controlled by an unscrupulous leader, could lead again to all the sufferings – moral and physical – of life under the Rákosi regime. The sole reasonably efficacious guarantee against that eventuality was an institutional system of government based on free elections and on more than one political party: hence the prime motivation of the demand for a multi-party government. When the demands of the Revolution are analysed in the specific historical-social context in which they were made, they show a remarkable unity in content, notwithstanding the diversity of their form. They testify to the power of the ideology to penetrate into the social consciousness of the widest masses, and to the impotency of that same ideology to transcend the range of national interests. The individual may be taught to think of his interests as determined by the interests of the nation, but he cannot be made to reject the interests of his nation for the interests of an international movement. This would be equivalent to asking him to give up his vested interests in the social collectivity for an intellectual abstraction – particular individuals may be capable of such altruism, but certainly not the entire mass of the people.

The universal implication of the Hungarian Revolution, clarified by the demands of the revolutionaries, is that it showed Marxism-Leninism unable to provide unity in the Socialist bloc. Diversity of thought, deriving from national peculiarities, cultural affinities, historical animosities, territorial claims and political traditions, came to the forefront of political action the moment the centre's control lapsed, or was even temporarily relaxed.

The Hungarian Revolution typified the nationalist transformation of the internally propagated ideological doctrine, and has convinced all partisans of the Soviet bloc who still entertained doubts as to the necessity of strong centralized control, that international Communism is unable to shed the totalitarian politics that originate from a common power centre, except at the cost of mushrooming ideological and institutional diversity leading eventually to friction and to revolt.

IV

THE DICHOTOMY OF CONTEMPORARY
POLITICAL THINKING

In schematizing the elements of political thought and the influences acting on its development we have reached the conclusion that particular historical-social conditions tend to favour the evolution of a primarily individualist, or a mainly collectivist pattern of thought. This analysis is devoted to an attempt to trace these "spontaneous" types of individualism and collectivism to origins in the major processes shaping the face of contemporary civilization.

For purposes of such a wide ranging analysis we may describe three processes as having had a primary role in making civilization what it is today. These are: (i) the industrial-technological-scientific revolution, (ii) the sharp upswing in the rate of increase of the world population, (iii) the emancipation movement of historically backward and oppressed masses on all continents. A definite causal nexus connects these processes. It is unnecessary to espouse a fully deterministic view of history to posit that each of the above processes has proved to be conducive for the development of the next by creating conditions which were on the whole favourable to its evolution. A form of chain-reaction, not excluding the interplay of several other factors and radically different processes, could thus obtain from the initiation of the industrial-technological-scientific revolution to the emancipation movement of great masses. This causal series of events had, as we shall attempt to show, the major role in producing spontaneous (i.e. not ideologically steered) tendencies for individualism and collectivism in our day.

The technical innovations of the Modern Age may themselves be traced to anterior factors, producing conditions which were favourable for such discoveries. For our purposes, however, it is hardly necessary to go back further than to the advance of the Modern Age and the general technological progress which heralded it.

The industrial-technological-scientific revolution (starting in the 17th century with the experiments of Galileo, and with Newtonian physics) had far reaching effects upon the course of history. As regards the evolution of political thought, this revolution was the cause of two major processes acting upon the thinking of men: (i) Through creating conditions, medicaments and practices to preserve and lengthen life it dropped the death rate, triggering off a population cycle that explosively increased the world population. (ii) It developed channels of communications among all people of the globe and brought to hitherto isolated areas the breath of civilization. Thereby it sowed the seed of civilized social consciousness and gave rise to political thinking in a world-wide context by people whose thought had not previously exceeded the limits of their immediate environment.

World population has steadily increased since the dawn of mankind, but its increase has not followed a constant curve. Rather, population growth has resulted in a series of upward steps, each being closely bound to some invention or improvement affecting the subsistence of the race.[1] Population growth appears to be intimately linked to technical advance, and the advent of the technological Modern Age has not failed to produce a corresponding effect. While the world's human population is estimated to have been at around 20 million in 3500 B.C. it had reached 100 million by approximately 850 B.C. It took humanity until 400 A.D. to reach the 200 million figure, and until 1650 to reach

---

[1] The chief stages in this process have been characterized by Julian Huxley as follows: "First, the food-gathering stage, as typified by the Australian aborigines before contact with white civilization. During this stage of human evolution, the maximum world population could not have exceeded a few millions. The invention of organized hunting, as practiced by Upper Paleolithic man or by the Plains Indians in their pristine state, would have allowed perhaps a doubling or trebling of maximum human numbers, though never any high density of population: the total population of North America east of the Rockies in pre-Colonial times is estimated at only about one million. The discovery of agriculture had a much bigger effect, and the two or three millennia of the neolithic revolution were marked by a great expansion in human numbers and by great movements of peoples.
The next major step was the step to civilization, with writing and large-scale organization of production, trade and administration, but still relying for its energy on man-power and beast-power, with a little tapping of wind and water. This permitted population to rise again, in spite of constant wars, recurrent famines, and occasional world pestilences such as the Black Death, to over 500 millions.
Then came the second really radical step – the harnessing of non-human power to human production, initiating the industrial, scientific, and technological revolution of the seventeenth to nineteenth centuries. This many-fold multiplication of power led to a spectacular multiplication of human beings. World population doubled itself twice over in the period between 1650 and 1920, and will have doubled itself a third time by the early 1980s. Further, while the first doubling took nearly two centuries, the second took well under one century, and the third will have required only about 60 years. Unless something wholly unforeseen happens, the world's present population will be doubled again within half a century."
Julian Huxley, "World Population," *Scientific American*, March, 1956.

540 million. Thereafter a sudden explosion took place, which rocketed world population to 2.200 million in 1950. The acceleration appears to follow certain characteristics, which are expressed by the term *population-cycle*. Phases of this cycle follow closely upon the level of civilization attained in a society. At a relatively primitive civilized level societies pass through a phase earmarked by high birth- and death-rates (the "High-fluctuating" stage). The introduction of civilization (hygiene, medical care, improved housing, better working conditions, etc.) has the effect of dropping the death-rate, while the birth-rate still remains steadily increasing (the "Early-expanding" stage). Hence as a first consequence of civilization, population increases sharply. Several generations of high-level civilization tend to deflate the increase by producing a decrease in the birth-rate (the "Late-expanding" stage). Since the death-rate continues to drop until it approaches a final limiting value, population is still increasing at this phase, but not as rapidly as before. The full effects of civilization then bring in a relative egalization of the birth- and death-rates (the "Low-fluctuating" stage). The Western world alone has felt the fullest effects of civilization and responded with a stabilized population level, increasing only at the rate of a fraction of one percent per annum. In this high and typically western phase of civilization the death-rate reaches 10% per 1000 and penetrates even below this figure (as in Holland) while two interacting factors restrict the increase of the birth-rate: (i) A high intellectual standard proves to be incompatible with very large families – many children tend to interfere with the enjoyment of the amenities of culture demanded by the intellectually evolved parent; (ii) High intellectual standard can seldom be maintained except for relatively small families: higher education costs money which the average parent cannot spend on many children. In competitive societies children are in many ways more of an economic drawback than an asset. Excessively large families weigh on the family budget to the point where the standard of the family's existence suffers. Hence high-level civilization cannot tolerate a rapid population increase, except at the cost of sacrificing some of its intellectual-cultural level – a cost which European societies appear to be unwilling to pay.

However, civilization has attained this level in few societies outside Europe – even the population of the U.S.A. is still rapidly increasing. Afro-Asiatic and Latin-American societies are in a phase of rapid expansion: death-control was introduced rapidly and efficiently, with the result that the average life-expectancy has greatly increased. As the intellectual level of the population has not reached the European level the birth-rate has still continued to increase, so that some of the newly civilized countries grow at more than twice the highest rate ever experienced in the West – they can double their population within thirty years.[1]

Hence the world population increased rapidly precisely in those areas which were backward in relation to the standard of existence typified by the technological age, and thus produced large masses of people who only recently (in historical perspective) came into contact with the European brand of civilization. Technical progress opened new channels of communication with these masses and made them aware of their own status among civilized societies. One of the resultants of the spread of civilization has been the development of a social consciousness in as yet immature intellects, patterned on the concepts of independence, equality, and full rights in the world-society of peoples. The more spectacular product of this type of political thinking was the great wave of decolonization, and the adoption of autonomous constitutions in all corners of the world. Another product (one that was less easy to discern) was that the type of political thought developing in many of these areas proved to exhibit a leaning toward collectivism, and could provide fertile ground for the spread of Communist ideas.

The collectivist tendencies of these masses, and the collectivism of Marxism-Leninism are not due to purely accidental factors. In fact, both varieties of collectivism – the one spontaneous, the other theoretical – can be traced to the advent of the technological age. While technical civilization brought the blessings and curses of European civilization to the outlying areas of the world, it produced a mass within European society, which found itself in a very similar position to that of the now emancipating masses of hitherto isolated lands. The European mass was technically an economic class, since it was carved out of the social body owing to the rapid industrialization process. This class – the proletariat – was as much the product of the new age as the masses of underdeveloped areas: technical civilization secreted the former by giving rise to the phenomenal development of heavy industry, while technical civilization produced the latter by

---

[1] In Ceylon for example DDT and an organized anti-malaria campaign dropped the death rate from 22 to 10 per 1000 in seven years. This drop took exactly ten times as long to achieve in England. The birth-rate is still increasing, however, and in 1957 the population was growing by 2.7 per cent per annum (quoted by Julian Huxley, *op. cit.*).

creating a great upswing in world population, and infusing western ideas into the minds of the newly civilized masses.

The status of the proletarian has *dropped* from a formerly higher level in the scale of civilized existence, while the status of the awakening masses of relatively backward areas *progressed* from a lower to a higher status. Notwithstanding their differing origins, characteristics common to both are the dissatisfaction centred around their existence, and the demands they make for the egalization of their status with those of other population layers. The proletarian, just as the politically and intellectually awakening inhabitant of formerly isolated areas, developed a social consciousness which was acutely aware of his relatively low status and gave rise to a form of political thinking designed to bring radical emancipation. The two types are not contemporaneous, however. The European proletarian is a mainly 19th century product, while the rise of the great masses of underdeveloped areas has taken place mostly in the 20th century.

Let us consider the type of thought that entered on the social scene through these masses, as a fresh political force. Their political demands were centred upon the egalization of their social position with other strata of the world's population. These groups were characterized, however, by an average level of intellectual development lower than that of the people from whose domination they wished to secede, and with whose status theirs was to be equated. The masses confronted a social order built on a kind of caste-system, where the caste was not necessarily determined by birth, but could also be given by the individual's level of civilization. Under all forms of aristocratic administrations, the governing principle is individualist, i.e., the better classes (better by virtue of birth *or* civilization level) are given privileged status, and rule by virtue of their intrinsically higher qualities. Aristocracies could be characterized by the basic political statement *who you are determines what you are;* – the being of the individual determines his social position, his public function, and hence also his social existence. Now the increasing political pressure of emancipating masses acted upon and moulded this hierarchy of being. The political dissatisfaction of the masses was primarily social, i.e., derived from a comparison of their social status with those of higher population layers. These layers were presented as composed of individuals enjoying a privileged position by virtue of incorporating a higher grade of *being*. The moment this intrinsic superiority was questioned, stratified social systems appeared unjust, and the road to emancipation was spontaneously and naturally envisaged to lie in the direction of an egalization of all public functions, through the removal of empirical factors of differentiation among social strata (private property).

This primal form of political thought can be termed "spontaneous collectivism." It equates individual being with social existence and holds all men to be equal. It thus attempts social reform by equalizing the value of all public functions. Spontaneous collectivism may be characterized by the political statement *what you are determines who you are*. Social existence is seen as primary (concepts of being are seldom distinguished behind the facade of social existence), and existence is to be equalized by collectivistic means: collective ownership of land and of the forces of production, and collective administration of the state apparatus.

The more radical the difference in the intellectual maturity-level of the emancipating layers from those with whom they are to be equated and to whose ranks they demand to be admitted, the less likely is it that the ontological principle of the ruling class will affect their thinking. It is precisely at that time and place where aristocratic individualism produces the greatest differences in social levels that spontaneous collectivism is the strongest. European societies witnessed an outbreak of such spontaneous collectivism among the ranks of the 19th century proletariat; we witness a similar outburst today in the underdeveloped and rapidly emancipating countries of the world. There is one great difference, however, between these events, and that is the relative numerical strength of the masses. In Europe they have never been more than one class among several others. At the stage where their oppression was the greatest and their average intellectual level the lowest, they could give rise to a series of socialist revolutions, but the general structure of European society's political thought was merely shaken by their numbers and was not permanently transformed. As a result the process of emancipation has taken place here with the continued use of individualism as the ontological principle of the social organization.

The course of history in Europe could be summed up by the political statement that all men are essentially equal, but are qualified for public functions to various degrees. Consequently *who you are determines what you are on a secondary, accidental plane, for essentially "you" are the equal of all others*. All men are alike, but they know different things to different degrees, and hence they occupy divergent positions in the social order. The ontological principle of individualism is kept – it applies to the basic being of man. The stratification of the social system has also been kept, but applies only to public functions. Members of every class and milieu are given equal chance to penetrate into all social strata, since their basic being is valid for every existence, needing only knowledge (physical skill and/or learning) to qualify for any public position. Owing to this form of egalization the oppressed European masses were assimilated into a stratified and yet equalized social structure by means of a political reform which transformed a form of aristocracy into a form of democracy; aristocratic individualism into democratic individualism. Proletariat is no longer a class of being in the West, but only a level of existence, a level which is determined by the knowledge and capacity of its members. Whoever acquires a higher level of knowledge is given the opportunity to change his social status correspondingly.

The emancipating masses of underdeveloped areas find themselves in a similar position to that characterizing the 19th century proletariat in Europe also insofar, as their social, economic, and cultural traditions are undergoing rapid change, making traditional views of societal and general reality progressively less capable of accounting for the new pattern of experience. The tendency is already pronounced (in some African areas particularly) to regard traditional views as mere superstition, and to adopt a truly "modern" *Weltanschauung*. The correspondence of traditional religious and secular modes and systems of thought with the basic premisses of individualism and collectivism is likely to be less determinant of the political orientation of these masses than their actual socio-economic conditions. The force of changed circumstances produces a vital motivation for action, removing at the same time the edge from any possible conflict with tradition that might obtain thereby. Continuity in popular thought cannot surpass continuity in general experience: where an insular pattern of experience is radically modified by the influx of new forces, there the ideas accompanying those forces will be dominant, regardless whether they form a direct continuity with tradition or whether a sharp break with the past occurs. Lack of continuity may act as a brake on the processes for a few generations, but can neither arrest them, nor change the course of their development. For this reason spontaneous tendencies toward contemporary individualism and collectivism are determined by the actual, experienced conditions of a given society, and are only conditioned by the harmony or discord of tradition with actual social reality. Proof of the validity of this assumption is that people of so entirely different cultural traditions as the European proletariat of the 19th century and the masses of the underdeveloped areas of the 20th, could, and mostly did, adopt collectivism as their outlook on society, when their actual social position designated collectivist methods as suitable for their political objectives.

The most trying period in the existence of the European proletariat has left profound marks upon the course of history, owing to the identification of sympathizing intellectuals with its cause. They succeeded in giving the spontaneous efforts of the struggling masses an explicit, theoretical form. A more or less accidental interplay of events led to the adoption of Marx's highly evolved theoretical system by Lenin, who was to have a major share in the emancipation of the underdeveloped masses of the 20th century. The collectivism of the 19th century European proletariat, largely exhausted by the beginning of the First World War, thus gave birth to a theory which survived it, and could serve (with suitable modifications) as the systematization of the ideas of the emancipating masses of the 20th century. Collectivism gained *systematic form* in the thought of Marx and Engels, and it gained *political power* in the hands of Lenin. A 19th century movement, itself exhausted, and in Europe successfully resolved by suitable social reforms, has opened the gate to the arena of world-politics for the thought of the emancipating masses. With that the construction of the Socialist system could begin.

The contemporary development of political thought is closely linked to the impact of Soviet power on world affairs, armed as it is with Marxist-Leninist ideology, and backed by more conventional weapons. The above discussed processes have prepared the ground for Soviet ideological conquest by producing socioeconomic conditions wherein a form of collectivism was either already shaping up or was ready to develop when systematically introduced. Russia was ripe for collectivism when the Tsarist regime fell. The extreme stratification of Tsarist Russia, based on the primacy of different grades of being, needed to be equalized. The overwhelming majority of the people was living in poverty, and had already refused to attribute privileges of social position to intrinsic superiority on the basis of noble birth and tradition. The concepts of individual being and social existence have been traditionally equated and the revolution was too sudden and too violent to question the validity of this equation. Later, when a democratization process similar to that having taken place in Western Europe half a century earlier could have occurred,

Marxist-Leninist ideology had already taken root. Egalization thus commenced by the revaluation of all public functions as the functions of equal parts to the social whole. *What you are is who you are* is the Marxist view, and this view became a basic element of the Soviet idea of society.

The original doctrine underwent qualification in practice and was "creatively" extended (i.e., re-interpreted) to fit new situations as they came about. The course of events necessarily involved situations which were unforeseen and required to be treated by a logic of their own. New generalizations emerged and crystallized then, and the ideology became better equipped to deal with an increasing variety of situations. In the course of time the Soviet Communist ideology became capable of handling not only societal situations inside the Russian borders, but also situations outside of it, regardless whether they did, or did not offer favourable terrain for collectivist ideas. By the end of World War II the Marxist-Leninist ideology was potent enough to transform every kind of political thought to collectivism, wherever Soviet power gave the ideological campaign *carte blanche*. It no longer required extreme social stratification to create collectivist atmosphere, but collectivist thought could be induced in every sphere of society through the concentrated use of an ideology which leaves nothing unexplained and tolerates no contradiction. Wherever the Communist organization could penetrate, and wherever it managed to come to power, the political thinking of society underwent rapid changes.

To effect and maintain this transformation, Communism requires an organization with highly trained personnel. The organization must be centralized; hence it is necessarily hierarchic. The leader decides and gives the orders, these are executed by lieutenants, who pass on subsidiary duties to persons lower down the organizational scale, and the operation is repeated until all layers of the population are reached. When we consider that Communism preaches systematic collectivism identifying existence and being in such a way that existence determines being, and that it requires a centralized organization to propagate, it will appear inevitable that an essential kind of hierarchy should obtain in the practice of Communist societies. The political statement of spontaneous collectivism *what you are determines who you are* is hypostatized by the ideology. As the ideology requires a large and centralized organization to propagate, "what you are" is graded from the function of the Party-boss to the simple worker. Since in Communist societies public function determines existence and existence determines being, a high-level functionary assumes a high-level of being as well. The "cult of personality" is merely an extreme form of the essential hierarchy of Communist societies. Thus in practice the theoretical equality of existence gives place to a hierarchy which re-instates the aristocratic hierarchy of being by implication, i.e. brings back the very order which Communism attempted to demolish.

V

THE IMPACT OF SOVIET IDEOLOGICAL
COLLECTIVISM

The schema developed in Part I of this essay permits the systematic formulation of the impact of Soviet ideological collectivism on the evolution of contemporary political thought. The postulate of this formula can be only as good as its premisses are, premisses which we have analysed, and which give the following components to be included in the theorem:

(i) The particular historical-social conditions obtaining in a given country and shaping its political thought.

(ii) The political programme of the government. (This programme corresponds to the people's wishes if popular political thought has been institutionalized. This is not necessarily the case, however.)

(iii) The collectivism of the Marxist-Leninist ideology, consisting of historical materialism as an idea of society, and dialectical materialism as a *Weltanschauung*.

(iv) Soviet military and economic power.

We have the following varieties of historical-social conditions to consider (broadly generalized): A. Socially *backward* areas (former colonies, economically underdeveloped countries with a pseudo-feudalistic structure, Dictatorships of the conventional variety, Oligarchies and Autocracies of any kind); B. socially *progressive* areas (societies where social reforms have taken place and have removed undesired stratifications from the social structure, either through democratic or socialist policies).

Soviet strategy is determined by whether a given country is in the direct zone of Soviet military and economic power, or whether it lies outside of it and is not necessarily dependent on Soviet military and economic support. The final goal is in all cases to establish and consolidate Soviet power, but the means to achieve this target vary. These can be resumed in capsule form as follows:

Given conditions A in a country *outside* the Soviet power zone, the Kremlin's foreign policy is geared to the diagnosis of the "phase" of that society's evolution, i.e. whether it is feudalistic, or already bourgeois. Most countries with a relatively underdeveloped socio-economic structure would be classified in the feudalistic category. Given the general level of social and economic development in the contemporary world, these countries are backward and ripe for social reforms, which in the Communist optic represent revolution. The revolution should be that of the bourgeoisie, and should have as its purpose to install the rule of the bourgeois class with the economic system of capitalism. Lenin insisted, however, that wherever a nation is on the brink of a social revolution (i.e. of large scale reforms) the actual regime is weak, making it possible for the progressive forces to join up with the bourgeoisie in overthrowing the regime, and then before bourgeois capitalism could be installed and stabilized, to overthrow the bourgeoisie and initiate the Dictatorship of the Proletariat.

Much that on the historical materialist view of social processes can be criticized, it must be admitted that the basic conviction that Communism has favourable terrain wherever large scale social restructuring is about to take place or is intensely needed, is on the whole, true. This particular configuration of economic, and social conditions produces a collectivistic reaction in the widest strata of the population, and the reaction is sufficiently strong to annull the restraining influence of conflict with cultural tradition – if not immediately, then in the long run. It is obvious that institutionalized collectivism is a relatively novel phenomenon on the scene of civilization. The tradition of all people has had more of an individualist than a collectivist content, excepting perhaps the primitive tribes of Africa, Asia and Oceania, whose immediate background has been collectivist (though of course on an instinctive, rather than on a rational level). Hence the spontaneous tendencies we find today, have developed *despite* a more or less salient clash with tradition, under pressure of the experience of unsatisfactory social experience.

Marxism-Leninism is first of all a rationalized ideological collectivism. It finds ready echo in all societies where a form of spontaneous collectivism has either already developed, or is ready to spring up when prompted. Although collectivism remains the major attraction of Communism, its ideology represents a complete system of thought which has various levels of harmony and discord with traditional beliefs and modes of thought, either paving, or else temporarily ob-structing the road toward the adoption of collectivism on the Marxist-Leninist blueprint. In Russia, for example, the acceptance of Commu-nism was helped along by the utopian thought of the Muscovite religion which became associated with almost all peasant revolts up to the end of the 18th century (the "Old Belief"). There was thus some aspect of continuity between traditional Russian ideas about a perfect society and the utopia of Communist society which eased along the adoption of the Marxist-Leninist version of collectivism. A similar continuity obtained in Asia in the regions where the Confucian intellectual tradition was dominant. The belief in the possibility of perfecting a social order is inherent in the Confucian tradition. Con-fucianism sought in religion not so much spiritual salvation, for its idea of a perfect society did not serve an other-wordly goal (as that of Buddhism and Christianity), as it aimed to develop a principle of reason to be superimposed upon a cosmic order as the Reason of the State. Reason, in a sense, was the heuristically functioning theoretical concept of Confucianism in the social sphere: as Paul Mus wrote, "Con-fucian Reason allows Humanity to be discovered in Man." [1] Thus in addition to socioeconomic conditions making collectivism readily acceptable, the very structure of the idea of Communist society, built as it is on a conception of harmony between cosmic and social order, appealed to the Asian mentality, and made for the smoother spread of Communism. It is more than accidental that the Communist sphere in Asia almost coincides with the Confucian cultural sphere in China, Korea and Vietnam, and that many of the Communist leaders have emphasized the continuity between Marxism and Asian cultural tradition.

Utopian epics (as that of Kesar, the hero of Tibetan and Mongolian epics) provided another aspect of continuity between traditional, and Communist ideas of perfect society, and happiness in communal existence. Buddhism itself has been described as essentially similar to Marxism on the plane of social ethics, letting the Buryat historian and revolutionary theorist Zhamtsarano declare that "Gautama Buddha had given the world an accomplished system of Communism." [2] These (and other) points of continuity have lent added impetus to the Communist movement in Asia, leading sometimes to the fallacious

[1] Paul Mus, *Sociologie d'une Guerre*, Paris, 1952, p. 255.
[2] Quoted by E. Sarkisyanz in "Marxism and Asian Cultural Traditions," *Survey*, August, 1962.

conclusion that Asian Communism can be explained by aspects of harmony alone. In doing so, however, the discordant aspects of Marxism are disregarded, aspects of which the western character of Marxism is a major factor. The traditional schism between occidental and oriental thought is sufficiently wide to prevent any resemblances on individual points from cancelling the foreign flavour of Marxist-Leninist Communism for Asians. That points of resemblance have been emphasized by tradition-conscious Asians themselves, must be due to a desire on their part to make Marxism acceptable and applicable for Asia. The primary motivation of this desire could be none other than the attraction of the principle of collectivism for the specific configuration of social and economic conditions obtaining in many countries of contemporary Asia.

The socioeconomic conditions characterizing Latin America are, on the whole, similar to the conditions and problems faced by many Asiatic nations. Cultural traditions are widely different, on the other hand. The difference between Asia and Latin America is reflected in the *rate* of Communism's spread on the two continents, while the similarity of the conditions is parallelled by the territorial *gains* of Communism in both areas, notwithstanding the rate of progress. Taking the short-term view, it would appear surprising how little success Communists have had in Latin America during the decades of their activity. All things being equal, Latin America would appear to have been ripe for Communism for some time, in view of the wide-spread poverty, unjustified social stratification, injured pride, and the general desire to see radical reforms initiated. The fact is, however, that aside from a few revolts and bids for power (having a nuisance value more than anything else), Communists were not able to gain ground in Latin America until the events in Cuba and the spread of Fidelism (which, outside of Cuba is still not fully identical with ortho-dox Communism). The answer to the riddle must be searched for in the atmosphere of Latin-American societies, of which cultural tra-dition, radical reformism, anti-American sentiment, and extreme nationalism are inherent components.

Of these only radical reformism (emanating from the unsatisfactory experience of actual social reality) provides favourable ground for Communism, since radical reformism is by nature collectivistically oriented. Anti-Americanism is favourable for the acceptance of a Soviet ideology on the *revanchist* principle of rebound. However, such tendencies are more than balanced by Latin-American nationalism: an adoption of Soviet methods would evidently bring with it a much tighter dependence on an extra hemispheric power than dependence on the USA, a hemispheric power, has ever involved. The cultural tradition of the continent, composed of Spanish and Indian elements, has little use for a totally foreign ideology. Nevertheless, the need for radical reforms is pressing, and actual experience pushes tradition increasingly in the background. The decisive point has been reached in Cuba: the intense need for radical reformism, fed by anti-American feelings, triumphed over cultural tradition and national pride in hemispheral independence: collectivism has been accepted on the Marxist-Leninist blueprint. Proportionately to the increase of the need for reforms, the power of Latin-American tradition to prevent the adoption of collectivism as the principle of state pales, and the potency of national pride for standing in the way of accepting Soviet methods and aid for making collectivism operational diminishes.

There have been attempts of late to trace parallels between Marxism and African cultural traditions: it has been pointed out that Marxism, through the syncretic powers of Africans, can lead to a return of the tribal type *Weltanschauung* at a level better adapted to the exigencies of modernized African existence than the traditional myths; that traditional African religions are nontheistic ritual systems, rather like Confucianism and thus harmonize with Communist atheism; that Islam, a major component of many African tribal traditions, is all-embracing, as Marxism, and Marxism could penetrate into the African consciousness, traditionally accustomed to see cosmic laws in everyday occurrences, with at least as much ease as Islam did; that in traditional African myths there are forms of dialectics between society and nature, many traditional cosmologies being markedly dialectical in character, founded on the necessity of conciliating and balancing opposites; that Marxist materialism is not opposed to African tradition, since the supernatural figures of myths signify merely imaginative representations of forces, and thus deal with material phenomena in a superficially theistic language.

Despite these points of harmony between traditional African culture and the Marxist-Leninist *Weltanschauung*, Communism has not been successful in Africa as a whole. There appear to be no significant African masses eager to embrace Communism in any area, with the exception of the Union of South Africa, where conditions non-typical of the rest of Africa prevail. The main reason in our view, that Communism does not catch on in Africa lies not so much with the harmony or discord of the traditional *Weltanschauung* with the Communist ideology (for these factors are temporal and never de termine, but only condition, the acceptance or rejection of Communism) as with the fact that the average African is not ready yet to embrace *collectivism*, and thus has neither need nor comprehension for the Communist ideology. We must consider that the traditional African mentality is dominated by concepts of being: in the African idea of society the collectivity is subordinate to the forces which enter into the being of each individual. As a result the social function of a person is not seen as determinant of his being, indeed, socially beneficent activity is considered to be without importance for the well-being of the individual: it is merely a means to gain a livelihood, and is to be disposed with whenever possible.

The being of the person is seen to be determined by factors which do not originate in collective existence, but involve the relations of the individual to natural and supernatural cosmic forces. Since different individuals are dominated to different degrees by various forces, several levels of being are distinguished by the African mind. In most cases a superior level of being is attributed to the white man, making him intrinsically different from Africans, rather than tracing the difference to his social position. As long as the hierarchic view of human being dominates in Africa, there will be no desire to see all men occupy equal positions in the social order, and collectivism as a principle of African society will be unimaginable to the majority of the population.

African traditions have prevented widespread dissatisfaction from arising with the Aristocratic-type stratification of many African societies, left over from colonial times when the intrinsic superiority of the colonizers was an unquestioned axiom in the eyes of the population.[1] However, Africa is rapidly industrializing, its people are coming into increasing contact with the people of the rest of the world and traditions pale under the impact of radically changing societal reality. The influx of technological civilization, together with an education programme which tends to regard tradition as mere superstition, conspires to rob Africans of their traditional *Weltanschauung*. For these reasons it appears to be a question of time only, before the hierarchy of being now dominant in the African mentality will collapse, leading to dissatisfaction, and finding expression in demands

---

[1] The failure of Soviet envoys to win even sympathy in much of Africa may be ascribed primarily to the fact that living much as the local population (a technique that produced splendid results in Asia) the agitators and technicians lost all respect in the eyes of the Africans: they lived below the intrinsic plane of the "white man."

for large scale reforms. When the African no longer believes in the intrinsic superiority of the white race he will find himself occupying a position in international society which will be in many respects similar to that of the 19th century European proletarian: he will consider himself the equal of all men, but be less qualified and have less opportunities (seen from the international viewpoint) than most. He will consider his traditions as superstition, but will not readily find a frame of reference indigenous to his environment, and capable of expressing his ideas on society. All around him the social scene will be in a constant state of transformation, and he will naturally ask, to where all the turmoil is leading. At the same time he will be acutely aware of the importance of the social structure in the life of the individual, and will tend to evaluate his environment in terms of what it can offer for him. Large scale social processes together with a subjective evaluation of human values lead to the assumption that society determines the individual, since it is the various social relations obtaining in a given social order that provide the individual with the fulfilment of his needs. Thus the socioeconomic conditions likely to develop in most African nations in the near future will prove to be conducive to collectivist thinking, just as conditions in many areas of Asia and Latin-America already are.

The specific features which in the long run *determine* the collectivist leanings of a people's political thinking, notwithstanding the conditioning influence of a possible clash between theoretical collectivism and indigenous cultural traditions, may be summarized as follows: (a) social stratification based on the assumed intrinsic superiority of some classes (where "class" signifies not only an economic, but also a racial, intellectual or cultural group) touching on the equality of basic human rights, (b) refusal of the underprivileged classes to acknowledge the intrinsic superiority of the upper strata, (c) Widespread Jacobinism, i.e. a radical reformist spirit dominating the minds and actions of the underprivileged groups, (d) a sufficiently low standard of existence to make the majority acutely aware of the importance a correct social order has for their lives.

These causal factors characterizing the countries with a socially and economically underdeveloped structure (conditions "A") act on the political thinking of its majority through the mediation of traditional patterns of thought, beliefs and concepts. The historical pattern of experience is modified by the evolution of socioeconomic conditions, and the osmosis of the old and the new pattern of experience produces a syncretic set of ideas which may radically transform, but does not completely break with the traditional culture of the historical society.

In the course of time the more salient conflicts between traditional modes of thought and the "ideology" of the new experience are neutralized, and inasmuch as the above conditions have not been essentially modified during that time, the main features of the emerging political thought are characterized by an explicit or implicit conviction that (i) social relations play a primary role in the life of the person, (ii) members of the upper strata are not intrinsically better, but gained their superiority owing to their privileged position in society, (iii) social position is determined by private property, and since social position determines the person, equality among members of a society can only be attained by expropriating the privileged, (iv) only the good of the collectivity can assure the good of the individual, and therefore whenever the interests of the collectivity conflict with the interests of a private person the latter's interests must be sacrificed without compunction, (v) a general "master plan" is a categorical imperative in the life of a society, lest the selfish strivings of particular individuals encroach upon the existence (and by implication also upon the *being*) of the representative majority.

In the process of the transformation of political thought historical tradition is a conservative, and social experience a dynamic force. Given conditions "A," therefore, the conservative force will be feudalistic tradition, and the concepts and thought patterns associated with it. The dynamic force will be the growing dissatisfaction with the social order, projecting to the traditional views as well. Where tradition conflicts with the theoretical structure of Marxist collectivism and where traditional views are firmly entrenched in the social consciousness, there Communism will have no immediate and direct appeal either as a doctrine or as a practical goal. Should tradition be capable of being analysed to common points of departure with Marxism, and/or be occupying a more superficial place in the social consciousness (or should the syncretic powers of the people [as in the case of Africans] be highly developed) socioeconomic conditions will make for the easier and faster acceptance of Marxism either on the theoretical, or on the practical political level. Communism can then penetrate, for the adoption of the Communist ideology brings with it a transformation of the idea of societal reality, resulting in the adoption of the Communist political strategy as well; while the acceptance of the political programme of Communism induces the adoption of its ideological superstructure. If experience fails to support tradition and lends validity to novel ideas, it is only a matter of time before the evolution of political thought reaches the point where the structure of the new ideology becomes acceptable as a rational and valid appraisal of reality, and where the political programme of radical reformism, using the collectivist principle is seen as optimally desirable, over and above the desirability of traditional practices. When this point is reached, the ground is mature for collectivism, both in practice and in theory. Since the only propagated theoretical authentication of collectivism as a principle of social organization is Marxism-Leninism, the equation *collectivism = Communism* is not questioned. It is assumed that collectivism *is* the teaching of Marx, Engels and Lenin, and that no theory other than historical materialism is capable of accounting for, and guiding collectivist social processes. Hence the attraction of Communism for these masses lies in its collectivism, notwithstanding certain intellectuals, who being in more privileged positions themselves, may find other aspects of the theory more to their liking. Socio-economically underdeveloped areas tend toward collectivism, and are offered Marxism-Leninism as the only "scientific" collectivist ideology. Communism can be readily accepted then as an explanation of societal and general reality, since its optic corresponds to the viewpoint of the masses, and serves to reinforce an already developing mentality. In the last count popular belief in Communism is belief in the radical transformation of unsatisfactory conditions. Owing to the equation of collectivism with Marxism-Leninism, and the second equation of Marxism-Leninism with the USSR (as its most qualified exponent) the spontaneous collectivism of an underdeveloped country can lead to its attachment to the Soviet bloc and to the consequent subordination of its proper interests to the imperialistic goals of the Kremlin. Soviet personnel infiltrates the country's institutions once its government has opted for Communism, and takes over as instructors and behind-the-scenes managers. Soviet supremacy in the new construction becomes a by-word, and it is not surprising then that the authority of the masters should spread to all areas of the national scene. Soviet power penetrates by virtue of the acceptance of Marxism-Leninism by sincere, and perhaps naive collectivists. Thus the "Leninist" formula of Soviet strategy is (where A stands for socioeconomically backward conditions, R for radical reformism, C for a predominantly collectivist spirit, I for the Marxist-Leninist ideology, and S for Soviet power): *When A, then R, then* (sooner or later, depending on the force of, and conflict with, tradition) *C, then I, then S.*

Let us consider now conditions B in a country equally outside the Soviet economic and military power zone. In the relatively advanced social and economic conditions of such a country no desires for radical reforms are manifested: popular political thought has been already institutionalized to some extent, and the people not only have a vested interest in the existing order, but feel themselves associated with its specific characteristics. Conditions B apply to the so-called "Capitalist" countries of the world, where economic and social progress has preserved the principle of individualism, and transformed it from the aristocratic form typical of feudalistic regimes, to its liberal, democratic form. As the order built on the democratic-individualist principle is generally satisfactory, necessitating reforms from time to time (but not, however, a holistic restructuring of the entire order, casting doubt upon its basic principle) the spirit of collectivism (signifying revolution) does not develop among the representative majority of the population. As a result the Communist ideology is deprived of its main attraction – "scientific" fully planified collectivism – and its other features (the introduction of a principle of cosmic rationality into the social order, chiliastic utopia, international brotherhood, the dictatorship of the hitherto oppressed) are not sufficiently attractive to the majority to compensate for the association of the ideology with a foreign power and for its subordination of individual values. As conditions B are not conducive for the development of the spirit of collectivism, the Marxist-Leninist ideology does not penetrate into the social consciousness, and Soviet power cannot penetrate *via* its ideology. The (negative) impact of Soviet strategy in this case is (when P stands for parliamentary reforms): *When B, then P, then $\sim C$, then $\sim I$ and $\sim S$.*

Now if a socioeconomically backward country (A) *enters* the Soviet power zone by virtue of factors other than ideological, Marxist-Leninist ideology will be applied to satisfy the need for radical reforms. There will be a marked tendency, alleviated only by the exigencies of power-political expediency, to institutionalize the political ideas of the Soviet leadership, subordinating the national interests of the country to the goal of consolidating the Kremlin's grip on the international Socialist movement. The ideology is presented as the only correct programme of reform, disregarding possible conflicts with the historical mode of political thinking in the area. As radical reformism tends to give rise to collectivism, and as Communist ideology reinforces this trend, conflict with tradition is soon eliminated, but the conflict of national collectivism and Communist international collectivism is likely to take its place. The formula of Soviet strategy is then (when T stands for tradition, and NC for national collectivism): *When AS, then R through I, hence ~ T, but eventually NC.*

It remains to consider the method of Soviet strategy with respect to socioeconomically advanced countries coming, for a reason other than ideological, into the Soviet power zone. These countries do not require radical social reforms, for popular political thought has already been institutionalized (to some extent). Nevertheless there is always room for social reforms in even the most advanced society. It is the task of the Communist ideology, propagated without contradiction by virtue of Soviet power backing, to convince the people that the type of social reforms they need is exactly that, advocated by Marx and Lenin. This involves the transformation of the national idea of society from individualism to collectivism, a transformation which can be effected by totalitarian ideological measures, given sufficient time. That the Soviets undertake to effect this transformation, i.e. the fact that they bother to indoctrinate an already colonized nation, shows their reliance on the Marxist-Leninist ideology as the strongest support of Soviet power. The ("Stalinist") formula of strategy is: *When BS, then I, then R, then C, (and eventually NC).*

While in backward countries the Communist ideology ushers in Soviet power, in advanced countries only Soviet power can introduce the ideology. While Soviet control of a country depends upon the balance of power, the Soviet ideology is not dependent on armed might, but can penetrate into all areas and find acceptance wherever its programme corresponds to an already felt need for social reforms. Hence while Soviet power is effectively counterbalanced and limited by the forces of the free world, the Soviet ideology is neither limited nor counteracted by any effective measure with the exception of the efforts made to point out its fallacies. These are negative efforts, however, and are impotent to counterbalance the attraction of the ideology for uncommitted and socially backward areas. It becomes increasingly evident that, unless the West expects to rely entirely on nationalist revisionism and the intellectual erosion of the Marxist ontological principle in order to weaken Communism and to restrict its expansion, it must offer positive propositions on the level of thought, and positive action on the economic and political plane, suited to the political thinking characterizing socially and economically underdeveloped areas.

VI

THE POTENTIALS OF CONFLICT RESOLUTION

An effective resolution of the conflict in the political thinking of different societies can only come about by a mutual *rapprochement* of the extreme forms of collectivism and individualism. Institutionalized collectivism is, as we know, controlled by Soviet power. It is thus subordinated to a specific theory, which insofar as its basic tenets are accepted without question, is dogmatic. Whatever flexibility it has is limited to the interpretation of the basic premises, and can only take the form of a gradual "declassification" of various areas of thought from the theory's sphere of application, and the increasingly wide meaning attributed to the original formulations. These processes are under way, even if they are as yet at an early stage. The *rapprochement* from the side of collectivism does take place, but it is considerably slowed down by the resistance due to continued adherence to the century-old main thesis.

There is no dogmatic insistence upon one set of concepts restraining the processes on the side of individualism. While the conservatism of the prosperous strata is evident, the eagerness with which the younger generation attacks the world issues of our day should not be underestimated. From the interplay of the two a steady, although by no means radical process takes shape, leading at first towards a lessening of the conflict, and later, if permitted to take its course, to a resolution of its major elements.

We shall summarize in three points our propositions for accelerating through rational and purposive effort, the effective and spontaneous process of *rapprochement* under way today.

(I) Acknowledgment of the conditional validity of the collectivist principle

Validity for any specific variety of political thought is conditional, i.e. each mode of thought is valid only with respect to the circumstances with which it was meant to deal. By analogy, however, its validity can be extended to circumstances that are similar to the ones which gave rise to the thought itself. The validity of every kind of political thought derives from the fact that one set of circumstances always tends to give rise to one mode of political thinking, that one namely, which can deal with the resolution of its problems the most directly. If and when that political thought has been institutionalized and has succeeded in changing the conditions which gave rise to it, then the new, changed conditions correspond for a time to the institutions. During this time the institutions become a conservative force. When conditions change further, however, institutionalized and popular political thought is gradually severed, and the institutions may be kept operative only by force. This is the reason for the dogmatization of the Marxian brand of collectivism by the USSR. But collectivism itself is not Marx's invention; it is a basic mode of approaching the resolution of social problems and is valid in those circumstances where collectivist measures are better suited to deal with them.

Wherever the terrain is suited for the rise of spontaneous collectivism, and wherever conflicts with historical traditions have been neutralized, Communist ideology can be effectively countered only with collectivism of a non-Marxist pattern.

Several new and still underdeveloped states are already building societies of a collectivist type, without following the Communist blueprint, and without benefit of the leadership of a Marxist-Leninist Party. This poses a serious challenge to the Communist ideology. If these nations succeed in developing an efficiently functioning and stable socialist-collectivist structure on a national, rather than on the Communist international blueprint, Soviet ideologists will have to redefine the processes of socioeconomic change. The success of such social constructions strikes at the base of the Soviet ideology and its dichotomic image of the world. Non-Marxian collectivism can neither be all black nor all white; it is difficult to classify it even as "revisionism," since it has not adopted the Marxist-Leninist doctrine in the first place. At the same time development of these social structures would break the Soviet monopoly on the principle of collectivism, and would make that principle open to all states without its adoption signifying an ideological and political commitment.

Now underdeveloped and rapidly industrializing nations are receiving both "socialist" and "capitalist" aid. Aid from the Socialist bloc comes with strings attached: through it Communists hope to transplant Marxist-Leninist ideology. There could not be similar intentions strung to "capitalist" aid, since the new social constructions are built on a non-capitalist socioeconomic pattern. Proportionately to the acceptance of Soviet bloc aid by these nations, grows the influence of the Soviet ideology in their institutions. The less they are dependent on "socialist" and the more on "capitalist" aid, however, the freer the local leadership can be to choose the nation's political orientation. While the truth of this proposition is generally acknowledged, the mutual mistrust of the western Powers and such underdeveloped nations due to the theoretical incompatibility of democratic and socialist principles stands in the way of the full success of the economic aid programme on the ideological level. As long as the West hands out aid primarily to *prevent* Communist influence in collectivistically oriented underdeveloped countries, the positive effect of the proffered support will be missing. The times require that the pragmatic compatibility of diverse socioeconomic systems be openly admitted, and be supported by a conception of social and economic change accounting for collectivism as for individualism as parts of an integral (and compatible) progression of societal processes. Doing so could result in the genesis of an increasing number of new and still underdeveloped states achieving "socialism" without entertaining ideological and political ties to the Soviet bloc resembling those of a pupil to his master, but developing and maintaining equal relations with all power centres. Not only would the ideological expansion of Soviet power (by means of the "Leninist" formula) be checked thereby, but the entire historical structure of the Soviet ideology would be shaken and require reinterpretation. By means of such "evolutionism" in the still backward areas of the globe, the national-revisionist tendencies of Soviet bloc countries would also be strengthened. The example of China and the majority of the East European Satellites has shown that the pupil learns fast and soon starts disputing the correctness of the thesis with his master. Communist internationalism tends to become transformed into Marxist-patterned national collectivism, and a Moscow-ruled Party structure is felt increasingly as a foreign body in the national organism. The result of Communist indoctrination is the development of a primarily nationally oriented Marxist collectivist (and of course noninstitutionalized) political thought. While popular political thought is collectivist, it sets national goals, and is anxious therefore to avoid foreign interference with the smooth progress of the projected construction. Hence the noninstitutionalized political thought is neutrally disposed, having for its prime objective the necessary freedom (given only by national independence) to construct on Marxist-collectivist principles. To dispute the validity of socialism as such, is to make adversaries of essentially nationalist peoples. The label of "counterrevolution" attached to the genuine nationalist movements of the Satellites only serves the Kremlin's purpose. No western "agents" have incited such revolts, and to claim that they have is an obvious falsification. It is a falsification proposed by the Soviet side, in an attempt to develop animosity toward the West. Communists know well that these uprisings do not aim at the reestablishment of the "bourgeois order of factory owners and landlords," and that few things could be more discouraging to the people than to find that their feelings have been exploited for ulterior and foreign purposes. The dissociation of Western interests from the western socioecomonic system through the inclusion of collectivism, in addition to individualism, into the acknowledged and valid principles of social organization could remove an otherwise unfounded animosity from the noninstitutionalized political thinking of Soviet bloc nations, and could effectively contribute to the emergence of national collectivism, wherever either the Soviet ideology, or historical-social conditions have oriented thought toward the adoption of the collectivist principle.

(II) The Perfecting of Democratic Individualism in socioeconomically advanced societies.

The transition from aristocratic to democratic individualism has been emphatically under way in Western Europe since the Socialist revolutions subsided in the middle of the last century, but its roots reach back to the first civic strivings prior to the French revolution, and have found expression in the writings of Rousseau, Locke, and other Social Contractists. The United States adopted democratic principles in its Declaration of Independence, and can thus continue the transition unimpeded by historical traditions, and aided by ideas inherited from the Anglo-Saxon world. Europe, on the other hand, has to transcend its established historical heritage at every step. The transformation from aristocratic to democratic individualism is by no means completed today. Many remnants of the characteristic features of European aristocracy still survive and condition contemporary life. Now the definitive characteristic of aristocracy is the stratification of the social system on the basis of the essential primacy of being: in Aristocracies, various classes of people occupy social positions according to the differences attributed to them as individuals. A member of the highest class, for example, belongs to that social strata because he was born into the milieu, and not because he has proved his superior abilities in a public function. Correspondingly, the member of the middle-level classes (the bourgeoisie, small landowners, etc.) belong to these classes primarily by virtue of their birth and milieu. The labourers and peasantry are also held to be the products of origins and environment, rather than of the efforts and capacities of the individual. In Aristocracies, the public function is equated with the individual being of every person, and his being is seen to determine his function. The pure form of democratic individualism on the other hand, removes the hierarchy of being, and permits existential stratification on the basis of various individual capacities for performing public functions. Since the dichotomy of being and existence is effected in democratic individualism, social existence is no longer determined by the individual's being, but by his capacity to perform a socially beneficent function. This, one of the high ideals of democracy, has not yet been fully attained. Two equations left over from former days are still operative to some extent. One is the tendency to regard certain people intrinsically superior to others (equating being and existence with being as essentially determinant of status); the other is to bring the social status of the public function over to private life (equating existence and being with existence as determinant of status).

The belief in the intrinsic superiority of some people to others finds expression in racism, but goes far beyond that extreme form, penetrating the fiber of even the most advanced societies. The placid, uncontested acceptance of a less capable man as social superior merely on the basis of his origins and milieu signifies an equation of being and existence with being as determinant of social position.[1] The acceptance of one race or nation as superior to an other by virtue of past achievements, reputation or any other factor, testifies to the equation of the two concepts of man on the *collective* level. Thus when a relatively underdeveloped country looks up to a more advanced people not only as a group of better trained, historically more favoured and therefore better qualified people, but also as their intrinsic superiors, a form of

[1] The only instance where intrinsic, inherited being still determines a high public function in an otherwise democratic society is the English *House of Lords*. The strong conservative spirit of the British people has undoubtedly been the major cause of the preservation of this practice. It is significant, however, that even that institution is losing power as a legislative body, and has assumed a more symbolic function.

international aristocracy obtains, which is in direct opposition to democratic principles.

Carrying over the status attained in public function to private life signifies the equation of being and existence with existence as determinant of status, and is therefore identical with the basic concept of collectivism. European societies appear to be less democratically evolved in this respect, than the United States.[1]

A separate study could be written about the significance of dress as a symbol of the process of transformation. In Aristocracies each class (meaning each class of *being*) wore a distinguishing habit. Members of every class could be identified at first sight, merely by their appearance. The soldier's dress was merely one uniform among all the others, each serving to emphasize the place of its wearer in the social hierarchy. The right to wear a certain kind of dress was not to be earned by individual effort (within certain, strictly defined limits), it was much more an inherited right and duty. Dress was merely the external symbol of intrinsic differences in the being of individuals: a count may have dressed up as a servant, yet he remained a nobleman; the servant's habit was not "his" dress, but only a masquerade. The modification of this outer symbol of social worth faithfully reflects the democratic transformation. The more advanced the transformation is, the more differences in dress are reduced, and the distinct habits of separate levels of being give place to a common "uniform" of democracies: a plain business-suit for men, and the current fashion for women. The work-cloth of factory workers, the white gown of doctors and nurses and the overall of farmers (etc.) is a functional dress used during the hours of work, discarded and changed for the "democratic uniform" thereafter. Only individuals whose public function requires that they be immediately recognized as functionaries of a public corps wear distinctive clothes: these are the uniforms of soldiers, policemen, transportation officials and the like.[2]

[1] To give two examples among many: the social status is carried over into private life by the German custom of addressing individuals in private life by the title of their public function ("Herr Doktor," "Herr Studienrat" etc.). The English conception of a "gentleman" comes also into this category today: a gentleman is recognized more by his education and his manners in our day, than by his origins. Once a gentleman, always a gentleman, i.e. the social function of a man qualifying him for this title remains with him in his private life also. There could be no objection to this custom if all men were considered to be gentlemen in their private life. All men are not gentlemen, however, in the eyes of the conservative British public.

[2] The power of distinctive uniforms to create the impression of an intrinsic quality of being can be seen when these contemporary wearers of uniforms change to civilian dress: their whole being appears to have changed from one specific type of functionary to men like all others.

The separation of private and public life is hampered by tradition in Europe, and could progress farthest in America: there the increasingly uniform dress of all levels of the population symbolizes the equality of all people as citizens notwithstanding the stratification of the public life.

A rational approach to the problem of accelerating the democratic transformation of society requires that its major phases and manifestations be clearly defined. If agreement could be reached concerning the basic principles of democracy, the entire sphere of social life could be examined in the light of common ideals, and rational measures could be introduced to smooth the way for the great but unevenly progressing social process: Western society's transformation from aristocratic to democratic individualism.

(III) Institutionalizing each nation's popular political thought

The major cause of the present ideo-political world conflict is dogmatic insistence on already superannuated political convictions, derived from the thought of past epochs. There is good evidence that the popular political thinking of all advanced nations approaches an increasingly similar idea of society. There are spontaneous movements to revise the official political dogma in the Socialist bloc, and there are equally spontaneous tendencies toward the removal of the extreme factions of the stratified social system in western democracies: corporate capitalism equalizes wealth and delegates power to more inclusive groups, trade-unions bring the voice of employees to bear on the management of the organization, and in some countries the nationalization of public utilities and the state operation of transportation facilities contribute to a democratization process which has much in common – on the level of popular thought and feeling – with the socialistic strivings of the Communist world. Every intellectual scheme disregarding the natural and spontaneous currents of history can only serve to slow its progress and to act as a brake on international conflict resolution. Intellectual political schemes, applied as dogmatic blueprints of social construction may be motivated as much by the sincere desire to fulfil the wishes of a people, as by antagonism to the principles of the opposite viewpoint. It is as yet little realized that uncompromising conflict resides in the arbitrary abstractions of leaders pitched against each other in the arena of world politics only, and not in the genuine political thinking of most of the world's advanced peoples. Political thought may be transformed from individualism to collectivism under full ideological pressure (as it could no doubt be transformed in the opposite direction as well), but democratic individualism and sincere national collectivism both aim at the construction of a social order capable of affording optimum satisfaction to all men. Their disagreement concerns the means of realizing a perfected society and stems from a divergent conception of societal reality. Individualists hold the individual (as a person living for himself, his family and his immediate circle) to be determinant of the shape of his society, and consider therefore that an improved social order is attainable by a better knowledge of the individual, of his nature, and of his needs and wishes.

Collectivists conceive of society as determinant of the person, and believe that a better future must be achieved through the construction of a perfect social organization, making the emergence of true human nature possible. Since society is a theoretical concept derived from the concept of man, and that concept is defined (in a political context) through a specific balance between the ideas of individual being and social existence, the nucleus of the East-West conflict lies already in the importance attributed to private being and public function in the life of the person. Since it is impossible to conceive of a representative member of any society either as a purely individual, abstract being, or as a fully socialized, entirely relational existent, and since the practice (if not the institutions) of most modern states tend to approach a common standard, the components of popular political thought, namely the ideas of being and existence, must also show a tendency to reach balance, cutting away the offshoots of extreme individualism as well as of extreme collectivism. Practice yields experience, and experience crystallizes as the popular idea of the relation of man to his group, providing thus the bases for an ontological conception of human society. This basic popular political thought is, in the final analysis, the ultimate determinant of the evolution of social processes. Doctrinaire insistence and dogmatic inflexibility can only slow, but not arrest the processes motivated by a basic thought which is itself the product of actual experience. To the degree to which popular political thought is institutionalized, the structure of all advanced nations will assume a similar form, corresponding to universally human reactions to the experience of social existence in modern, technological civilization. Sincere and dedicated statesmen, regardless whether they are Democrats, Socialists, or Communists, have the good of the people at heart. Giving validity to the basic premises of public opinion by institutionalizing the form of political thought which is that of the majority in their country, would correspond to their fundamental objectives, since they could thus build or improve the type of society desired by the people. The institutionalization of popular political thought is the essence of the terms "Democracy" and "Socialism," and is consistently refused only by the dictators of aristocratic and oligarchic regimes.[1] Institutionalizing popular political thought is not only concordant with the highest ideals of all sincere statesmen, but it is also the surest way to reach a resolution of ideological conflict. The elimination of dogmatism and inflexibility in doctrinaire and tradition-bound politics, and the adoption of policies and objectives corresponding to, and derived from popular reaction to actual conditions, can contribute to the improvement of relations between states of different structures, and can, in the long run, lead to the elimination of conflict between the adherents of individualism and collectivism.

---

[1] That totalitarian dictatorships use the concepts of Democracy and Socialism signifies that their use of these terms is merely nominal, camouflaging profound disregard and contempt for the needs and opinions of the wide masses.

INDEX

abstraction 15, 16, 17
apprehension 13
Aristocracy 49–51
Aristotle 42, 43
Autocracy 49–51

Being *see* individual being
Bochenski, J. M. 108
Brezinski, Z. K. 55, 95, 99
Buchholz, Arnold 64, 108
Buddhism 153

Chen, Th. H. E. 107
class 36, 37, 50, 75, 82
Collectivism, def. 6; as idea of society 28;
    as principle of organization 46, 47, 52–
    57, 82, 169, 170; ideological 148–161;
    metaphysical 73–75; national 94–101,
    111–140, 161, 164, 165; popular 88–110;
    spontaneous 144–148; validity of 82–86,
    162–165
collectivist theory 28, 34–37
collectivist state 52–57
comprehension 13, 21, 23; objective 16,
    21–25, 38, 41; subjective 16, 21–25, 38,
    41, 66, 68, 72
Communism 4, 40, 47, 63–86
Communist ideology 8, 63, 64, 85, 95, 105,
    149, 163–165; impact of 151–161
Communist Party(ies) 87, 88, 90, 103, 106,
    149
concept 13–15, 20, 21
concrete being 6
concreteness 5, 17
conflict, ideological 87ff.
Confucianism 153
Conservatism 35–37
content of political theories 31, 36
CPSU *see* Communist Party

Democracy 4, 49–52, 147, 165–170
Democritus 65, 66

Dialectical Materialism (Diamat) 79, 80,
    91, 92, 99, 107–109
dialectical materialist epistemology 72
dialectics, Hegelian 45, 69, 73–75; in
    Communist strategy 82, 90, 94, 95; in
    nature 81; in theory of knowledge 72;
    Marxian 45, 69, 74, 75
Dictatorship of the Proletariat 54
Dictatorship, totalitarian 55–57

East-European Satellites 94–96, 111–117
Engels, Friedrich 45, 64, 75, 79–81, 148
Epicurus 42, 65, 66
epistemological problem 10, 11
essentialism 11
existence *see* social existence
existential relations 5, 28
experience, of society 5, 11, 58; satis-
    factoriness of 35–37

Fascism 52–54
Feuerbach, Ludwig 66
Friedrich, C. J. 55

Hegel, G. W. F. 45, 65–75
heuristic concepts 27, 31, 39, 42–45, 48, 52
hierarchy, social 49, 57, 145, 148, 157, 166
Hitler, Adolf 53
Historical Materialism (Histomat) 79, 91,
    99, 108
historical-social factors 30–37, 39, 83, 87
Hungarian Revolution 115–140; demands
    of 118–130

ideology, def. 7, 8
Individualism, def. 6; aristocratic 49–50,
    145, 165–168; democratic 50, 51, 165–
    168; as idea of society 28; as principle
    of organization 45–51, 165–169; onto-
    logical 70
individual being 5–7, 9, 12–19, 32, 41, 46,
    49, 57, 88